BERLITZ®

SYDNEY

- A ✔ in the text denotes a highly recommended sight
- A complete A–Z of practical information starts on p.109
- Extensive mapping throughout: on cover flaps and in text

Although we make every effort to ensure the accuracy of the information in this guide, changes do occur. If you have any new information, suggestions or corrections to contribute, we would like to hear from you. Please write to Berlitz Publishing at the above address.

Text:	Ken Bernstein
Editors:	Sarah Hudson, Giles Allen
Photography:	Claude Huber (p.37 NSW Tourist Commission)
Cartography:	(cover flaps) Falk-Verlag, Hamburg
	(interior) MicroMap
Thanks to:	The Sydney Convention and Visitors' Bureau for their invaluable help in the preparation of this guide.

CONTENTS

The City and The People

With a setting as winning as San Francisco's and a lifestyle that even Californians admire, Australia's biggest and most cosmopolitan city might just strike your fancy. It can't be a mere coincidence that one out of every five Australians chooses to live in Sydney.

Brassy and sassy, Sydney is like a spoiled brat who knows he's got it all, including money and looks. Skyscrapers humming with financial and industrial power look down on a fabulous, sunsplashed harbour. Even though Australia's tranquil capital, Canberra, is the seat of government, Sydney is the palace of the economy and the media.

In spite of Australia's rather out-of-the-way location in global terms, the biggest industry to generate foreign exchange is tourism. Every year well over two million foreign tourists head Down Under, and most of them head for the south-east coast for a glimpse of Sydney.

Sydney's 3½ million inhabitants, who tend to be friendly and witty, know the city has everything anyone could ask for, tangible or inspirational or flighty. After work – and Sydneysiders live for the leisure hours – there is a choice of every cosmopolitan delight imaginable. It's a sunny coincidence that over 30 beaches famous for surfing and scenery are only minutes away. And escaping to the Outback is a mere day trip; you only have to travel beyond the suburbs to see your first 'Caution – Kangaroos' sign.

The Nation's Birthplace

Military strategists have always longed for an anchorage like Sydney Harbour. For a couple of centuries, ever since the first settlers here stumbled ashore at Sydney Cove to construct a new nation, the harbour has been entirely stealing the show.

5

Most of the world's great cities have a landmark – an Eiffel Tower or a Golden Gate Bridge – which serves as an instantly recognizable symbol. Sydney has two, both built on the harbour: the perfect arch of the Harbour Bridge and the billowing roofs of the Opera House. That's the result when both engineers and architects embellish a haven coveted by artists and admirals.

It's a pity Captain Cook never really noticed the glorious setting of Port Jackson (the official name of Sydney Harbour). He gave it a glance, and its name, as he sailed past on his return in 1770.

One of the specialists on Cook's ship *Endeavour* was the naturalist Joseph Banks. He felt that Botany Bay could be the site of a penal colony, badly needed to relieve the overflowing prisons in Britain. His version of a continent crying out for development turned out to have been something of an exaggeration, for the territory could hardly have been more hostile; the 'meadows' he described were more like swamps, and the land was best suited for growing rocks.

Hostile, too, were the natives, understandably less than pleased at the casual seizure of land that had belonged to them for tens of thousands of years. The dark-skinned semi-nomadic hunters who met, or more usually avoided, the new arrivals, were still in the Stone Age. They probably then numbered 300,000. Now the Aboriginal population of Australia has dwindled to about two-thirds that number. No easy answers have been found for their problems of adjustment to the white society around them, but the government persists in attempts to right a lengthy list of wrongs.

Founding Fathers

In 1788, when the First Fleet delivered the new country's first 1,500 colonists to Sydney Cove, more than half of them were convicts. Something like 160,000 jailbirds were to follow. You can get a feeling of the early days of New South

Wales walking through The Rocks, Sydney's first commercial and maritime neighbourhood. They've restored many of the early 19th-century buildings, and widened the viaduct chopped through the solid rock by chain gangs. A couple of the earliest pubs are still in operation.

The fact that the majority of the founding fathers were convicted felons rather than firm-jawed idealists has undoubtedly had an effect on the national psyche. Does the family tree account for the imaginative, cockney type of English spoken by Australians of all classes and regions? Is today's social mobility and sense of egalitarianism a direct reaction to the early days of keepers and convicts? And does the macho tradition stem from the scarcity of females in the young colony?

Australians in general have tended to be insecure about their roots, though pride in convict ancestors has become more stylish in recent years. Whatever the genealogy, the typical suntanned Sydneysider

Sydney's office workers relax through lunch. In fact Australians make the most of all leisure hours.

brims with self-confidence. A notorious slogan of the 1980s thumbed the city's nose at the rest of Australia and, for that matter, the world: 'If you're not living in Sydney, you're camping out.'

The city undoubtedly has sensational advantages, but let's be realistic: just as more New Yorkers live in Queens or Brooklyn than glamorous Manhattan, most Sydneysiders live in areas far from the bright lights or the beautiful harbour views. Sydney is no more typical of Australia than Manhattan is of America.

The Descendants

When you want an example of urban sprawl, think of Sydney. The city covers 4,075 sq km (1,573 sq miles) – more than three times the area of the famously expansive city of Los Angeles. However, it is very pedestrian-friendly, with many worthy sights either in the central district or at least within walking distance of it. **8** The suburbs, smart or quaint or downright grim, are served by a comprehensive network of buses, trains and ferries.

The statistics seem made to measure for people who are, well, somewhat on the frivolous side. City-slickers or suburban dwellers, the Australians are fanatics of the outdoor life. They radiate rude health and tanned muscles. If they're not actually down at the beach, they'll probably be out hiking, jogging or playing Aussie Rules football, or you'll find them out in the garden barbecueing huge slabs of beef.

For visiting Americans, Australians seem quite English, while British newcomers are reminded of America. The informality and pioneering spirit Down Under do recall the American style, while the social and economic preoccupations and the attitudes to food more often lean towards the British. The Australian language might occasionally baffle English-speakers from almost anywhere, but it's admirably ingenious, and certainly as good-humoured as the Aussies themselves (see the cover of this guide for a few useful expressions).

As for culture, the average Australian might find the word itself rather tedious, maintaining that television and sports are culture enough. But don't you bet on it, mate! Go to any bookstore, or to any theatre showing a locally produced play or film and you'll see that all along a varied, challenging front, Australian creativity is thriving. For the tourist, Australia is the chance to combine treasures of art with nature's wonders, ballerinas as well as kangaroos. Everything, in fact, but ancient palaces and churches. In Australia, the most historic local monument is likely to be the jail (or gaol).

Superlatives

Australia is the earth's biggest island – and the least populous (16.5 million inhabitants) of the continents. It occupies about as much space as the 48 mainland states of the USA, or 24 times the area of the British Isles.

The flattest continent, the terrain of Australia hardly ever rises above middle-ranking hilltops. But the nation's summit, Mount Kosciusko (2,228m/7,316ft) is almost as high as Mexico City. Come down to earth at salty Lake Eyre, the continent's lowest point, 16m (39ft) below sea level.

Australia is the driest continent, the mass of its interior a parched blotter of desert. Although the Murray River and its tributaries add up to a Mississippi in length, few other rivers can house much more than a rowing boat. And many of the blue squiggles on maps are just sand traps for part of the year.

The coastline is the least ruffled of all the continents, a circumference of 36,735 km (almost 33,000 miles) devoted to sweeping beaches rather than coves and creeks. Here you can dip a toe, or a surfboard, in legendary seas and oceans, among them the Coral Sea, the Timor Sea and the Indian Ocean.

9

Beyond Sydney

After you've seen the Opera House, The Rocks, Darling Harbour, Chinatown and some of the other distinctive quarters, it's time to get out of town. Day trips lead to the beautiful Blue Mountains and scenery you'll find nowhere else; to the Hawkesbury River recreational region; to the wine country of the Hunter Valley, and beyond. All of these varied attractions belong to Australia's first state, New South Wales, of which Sydney is the capital.

New South Wales occupies about one-tenth of the conti-

nent's area. It packs in everything from dairyland and vineyards to desert and craggy mountains. An area six times the size of England is home to 5½ million people: cowboys and coal miners, sailors and scientists, trendy media types and some of the world's most relaxed beachcombers.

New South Wales covers a lot of latitude and altitude, from the country's tallest peak (Mount Koskiusko – see p.85) to desolate desert. But where the land is fit for cultivation, something will be growing: bananas, cotton and sugarcane in the north; apples, cherries and wheat in the south.

A homely atmosphere pervades at Bondi (left). In the city centre, old is reflected in new.

A Brief History

From the point of view of the original Australians, the sudden arrival of a fleet of colonists in the southern summer of 1788 was bad news. The newcomers, led by old-fashioned imperialists, had no sympathy for sitting tenants and simply broke their lease.

The Aborigines insist they were here all along, from the birth of the earth. More cautiously, modern scientists have carbon-dated a human skull found in the New South Wales Outback and pronounced it nearly 40,000 years old; when pressed, some authorities take the story back an additional 40,000 years.

The first inhabitants may have walked most of the way to Australia during the Ice Age from somewhere in South-East Asia. They had little problem adapting to the new environment. Accustomed to foraging, they found wild honey, berries and roots aplenty, and, for a change of diet, they were quite capable of spearing a fish or

All Ashore

First impressions are important. At Botany Bay, Captain Cook led a small landing party to check out the terrain and the people. Later he described the Aborigines he met with considerable warmth, but the truth is that he had to shoot his way ashore on that historic Sunday, 29 April 1770.

'As we approached the shore,' his private log reports, 'the natives all made off, except two who at first seemed resolved to oppose our landing. We endeavoured to gain their consent to land by throwing them some nails, beads, etc., ashore, but this had not the desired effect; for, as [we] put in to the shore, one of them threw a large stone at us, but [after] the firing of two or three muskets loaded with small shot, they took to the woods, and we saw them no more.'

Welcome to Botany Bay!

knocking out a kangaroo with a boomerang.

'The Dreamtime' is the all-purpose name for everything that came before them. It puts Aboriginal history, traditions and culture under one mythological roof. The Dreamtime's version of Genesis recounts how ancestral heroes created the stars, the earth and all the creatures. It explains why the animals, insects and plants are the way they are, and how the human race is able to live in harmony with nature. When Aborigines die, they are recycled to the continuum of the Dreamtime. Every tree, rock and river has its own mystical significance.

So when the newcomers from England came and seized the land, it was more than just soil they were grabbing.

*P*roof of early inhabitants decorates cave walls.

Voyage of Discovery

The written history of Sydney starts with Captain Cook. In 1770, on a trip back to England from Tahiti, the great British navigator landed on the east coast of Australia. Aboard his ship, the *Endeavour*, were two naturalists who found so many fascinating specimens that Cook was moved to name the place Botany Bay.

Although the Dutch and probably the Spanish and Portuguese had been to Australia **13** before him, Cook claimed all the territory he charted for King George III and coined the name New South Wales. Returning to London, he gave glowing reports of the continent he had glimpsed: a vast, sunny, fertile land, inhabited by Aborigines who were 'far happier than we Europeans'. The captain's positive thinking about 'noble savages' was to be the death of him. A few years later, on the island of Hawaii, he was slain and dismembered by a mob of angry Polynesians.

What finally put Australia on the front burner in the kitchen of British colonialism was the Boston Tea Party. In the 18th century, troublesome convicts had been banished to North America. After the American Revolution, this desirable destination had to be dropped. The prisons in Britain could not cope, and the supplementary floating jails threatened riot and disease.

The idea of a colossal British version of Devil's Island Down Under seemed somewhat far-fetched and expensive, but, since nobody had a better idea, in May 1787 His Majesty's Government began deporting criminals to Australia. In those days even amateur lawbreakers such as petty larcenists, bigamists and army deserters faced exile. Youngsters who had stolen an apple found themselves being transported to Australia. The programme lasted for 80 years.

Founding the Colony

Captain Arthur Phillip, a retired naval officer, was given command of the First Fleet, a low-budget expedition into the almost-unknown. Eleven sailing vessels carrying nearly 1,500 people, more than half of them convicts, set sail from Portsmouth, destination New South Wales. The ships' crews and prison officers had time to recuperate from the rigours of life at sea during resupply stops in the Canary Islands, Cape Town and Rio de Janeiro, but the prisoners did not set foot on land throughout the

A century of architecture reveals a nation still developing.   **15**

eight-month voyage. Remarkably, every one of the ships finished the trip and the death rate was only around three percent.

Under his new title of Governor, Captain Phillip rowed ashore, unarmed, and in full ceremonial dress. Spear-toting natives milled about, but nothing untoward occurred. One of the lieutenants on the flagship wrote: 'I think it is very easy to conceive the ridiculous figure we must appear to these poor creatures, who were perfectly naked.'

Unveiled at the same time was the bleak truth about Botany Bay. Captain Cook's rosy claims faded fast when it was discovered that there was no shelter from the east winds, that much of the apparent grassland was actually swamp, and that there wasn't enough fresh water to go round.

Luckily, the next best thing to paradise was waiting just around the corner. Governor Phillip took a reconnaissance party and sailed 12 miles further up the coast to discover what the Fleet Surgeon John White called 'the finest and most extensive harbour in the universe'. We call it Sydney Harbour. The fleet reassembled at Sydney Cove on 26 January 1788 (the date is recalled every year as the Australian National Holiday), and the British flag was raised over the new colony.

Although Captain Phillips decreed peaceful coexistence, his underlings were hostile or

---

A Ghastly Journey

The journey of the First Fleet is enough to make even an old salt seasick. By modern standards, the prisoners' living conditions on board the motley flotilla were inadequate even for animals – overcrowded quarters, little light or air, insufficient food, water and sanitation, vermin, and flogging for misbehaviour.

As it happened, animals were also aboard. Cattle, horses, pigs, sheep and poultry were all on the ship's manifest with yet more smuggled aboard by crewmen.

at least insensitive to the native population. Sacred Aboriginal sites were trampled and Aboriginal food and property were stolen; the natives retaliated with force and the colonists replied in kind. Violent incidents continued for years.

The Undaunted

Britain's expectations for New South Wales soon shrivelled in the summer sun. The soil was unpromising, and even if they had wanted to pitch in, most of the convicts were city-bred and could not tell the difference between a hoe and a banana. Many were also ill after the voyage, or too old for heavy physical work, and almost all were untrained in any useful trade. Livestock died or disappeared. Hunger and famine lurked as a permanent danger.

For nearly two years, delays from the London end and shipwrecks en route frustrated relief shipments. As food supplies dwindled, rations were cut. Prisoners caught stealing food were flogged. Finally, to set an example, the governor ordered the execution of a food-looter.

In June 1790, to all-round jubilation, the supply ship *Lady Juliana* reached Sydney Harbour, and the long fast ended. As agriculture finally began to blossom, thousands of new prisoners were shipped out to Australia. Soon even voluntary settlers were choosing Down Under as the land of their future.

When Governor Phillip retired, the colony's top army officer, Major Francis Grose, took over. His army fared very well under the new regime, which encouraged free enterprise. The officers soon found profitable sidelines, usually at the expense of the British taxpayers, with a monopoly on the sale of rum making them quick fortunes.

Reports of this racketeering prompted London to send out a well-known disciplinarian to shake up the colony. Captain William Bligh, the target of the notorious mutiny on HMS *Bounty* seven years **17** earlier, intended to put fear into the hearts of backsliding officers, but his temper was uncontrollable. His New South Wales victims nicknamed the new governor Cali-gula and plotted treason.

As the colony was toasting its 20th anniversary on 26 January 1808, a group of insurgent officers deposed Captain Bligh and held him prisoner for months. The Rum Rebellion, as the mutiny was called, led to a radical reorganization and reshuffle in personnel. But members of the inevitable court martial seemed to understand how Bligh's hard-line methods had galled his subordinates and the Sydney mutineers were given less of a punishment than they might have expected.

A New Deal

Under the progressive rule of Governor Lachlan Macquarie, New South Wales began to exchange the stigma of a penal colony for the aura of a land of opportunity. The idealistic Scottish army officer made a real town out of the shambles of Sydney. Replacing former mud-covered, thatched huts along paths that were either dusty or muddy, he set in motion the building of schools, churches, a hospital and court-

---

Bligh of the Bounty

History was unkind to Captain Bligh. In spite of all his achievements, he was stigmatized as a cold and petty autocrat.

When the *Bounty* mutineers, preferring Tahiti to home, set Bligh adrift in mid-Pacific, he applied great fortitude and navigating skill to survive 2,250 km (3,600 miles) in an open boat.

After the Rum Rebellion (see above), promotions enhanced Bligh's career and in 1814 he became Vice-Admiral. A bronze statue of this famous man of the sea, in rather Napoleonic pose, stands in The Rocks.

house. Almost all of his civilizing efforts were carried out against the wishes of his superiors in London. They wanted a spartan Australia as a permanent reminder to the convicts that this was punishment, not a brave new world.

To inspire exiles to go straight and to win emancipation, Macquarie appointed an ex-convict as Justice of the Peace, and invited others to dinner, to the horror of the local élite. One of the criminals the governor pardoned, the forger Francis Greenway, became the colony's prolific official architect. London was furious to discover, too late, the elegance of his buildings.

London prescribed tougher punishment, along with the total separation of prisoners from the rest of the population. All this led to long-lasting conflict between reformed criminals on one side and a privileged class of voluntary immigrants on the other. Nowadays, descendants of those First Fleet prisoners often express a kind of perverse pride in their heritage.

For Governor Macquarie and his immediate successors the biggest problem was the most obvious: although in a seaside location, the colony was hemmed in by mountains and there wasn't enough land to provide food for the ever expanding population. Every attempt to break through the steep valleys failed. Then, in 1813, an unconventional idea struck the explorers Gregory Blaxland, William Wentworth and William Lawson: they decided to take the high road, crossing the peaks rather than the vales. It worked. On the far side of the Blue Mountains they discovered a land of endless plains that would readily support a new society.

Other explorers – mostly surveyors, army men and keen colonists, with assistance from the convicts and Aborigines – opened the way for yet more new settlements like Brisbane, Adelaide and Melbourne. The authorities in London began looking for new sites for penal colonies – places so dreadful that Sydneysiders would be encouraged not to transgress. **19**

But most of the areas they discovered were full of promise. Voluntary settlers soon outnumbered the convicted exiles and between 1825 and 1850, New South Wales alone received 70,000 new settlers. Life there became so civilized that the University of Sydney was founded in 1850.

Age of Gold

Fortune smiled on Australia with sudden warmth in 1851. Beyond the Blue Mountains, about 130 miles from Sydney, near Bathurst, a veteran of the California gold rush, Edward Hargraves, found what he'd been looking for – gold.

He named the place of his discoveries Ophir, after the site of a phenomenal gold strike during the days of King Solomon. Virtually overnight, Sydney suffered a drain of able-bodied men rushing off to make their fortune.

Within months of the bonanza at Ophir, prospectors from Melbourne struck gold at Ballarat. The news of this

attractive boom in two colonies – New South Wales and Victoria – triggered an invasion of excited adventurers from Europe and America. By 1860 the population had in-

creased to a vast one million. Thirty-three years later the enthusiasm spread from the east coast to the west as gold was later discovered in Kalgoorlie, Western Australia.

There are vastly more sheep than anything else in the Australian Outback. Don't go there for lively conversation.

Life in the gold fields was rugged, aggravated by an accumulation of water shortages, the climate, the flies and tax collectors. In 1861 a riot pitted white prospectors against Chinese miners, who were resented for being foreigners, and for working too hard and spending too little.

At Lambing Flat, New South Wales, a mob of thousands of whites whipped and clubbed a whole community of Chinese. Police, troops and even the courts dealt leniently with the misguided aggressors. It was the worst of many race riots in the gold fields.

With the tensions of the gold rush came the notion of the 'yellow peril', quickly embedded in Australia's national conscience. Feelings ran high and strong and 'White Australia' immigration controls were to remain in force from 1901 until 1972.

Transportation of convicts to New South Wales was abolished in 1840 and finally ended for the whole of Australia in 1868, when London was forced to admit that the threat of exile to a golden land of sunshine and opportunity was not exactly a strong deterrent to crime.

The Bushrangers

Highway robbers, horse thieves and assorted outlaws fanned out across Australia in the 1850s; the gold rush served to make the stakes much more interesting.

Among the most notorious rogues was Ned Kelly. A one-time cattle rustler, Kelly led a gang which pulled off spectacular robberies, mostly in Victoria. His most memorable incursion into New South Wales was in 1879, when the gang kidnapped the entire population of Jerilderie, New South Wales, while trying to make a getaway after a bank robbery. A year later, as thousands mourned, an unrepentant Ned Kelly went to the gallows.

The New Century

With the blessing of Queen Victoria, the colonies of Australia formed a new nation, the Commonwealth of Australia, on 1 January 1901. This federation retained the Queen as Head of State, and bowed to both parliament and the privy council in London.

Loyalty to the British Empire was twice put to the test, and more than amply proven, in both World War I and II. A day before Britain declared war on Germany in August 1914, Australia offered an expeditionary force. Less than three months later, 20,000 Australian and New Zealand troops sailed to combat. On 25 April 1915, the Anzacs landed at Gallipoli. Doomed by bungled planning and keen Turkish defences, about 8,000 Australians died and a further 20,000 were wounded. Later, the survivors were deployed in the trenches of France, where casualties were even heavier but less dramatic. By the end of the First World War, more than 200,000 Australians –

about two-thirds of the entire expeditionary force – had been either killed or wounded. The death rate was the highest in the empire.

Between the wars, Sydney devoted its energies to building the Harbour Bridge, opened during the Depression days of 1932. The northern suburbs took on a new life, and the city's population passed the million mark.

In World War II the fighting came a bit closer. Japanese bombers attacked Darwin 64 times, enemy submarines penetrated Sydney Harbour, and invasion was perceived as a very real threat. Nearly a million Australians went to war but the ensuing casualties numbered far fewer than in World War I. Poignantly, almost one in three Australians held prisoner by the Japanese died in captivity.

After the war, Australia was transformed. Now psychologically involved with Asia, and feeling vulnerable, the nation developed a greater dependence on the United States than on Britain with ANZUS, **23** a defensive alliance of Australia, New Zealand and the United States founded in 1951.

Sharing the anticommunist stance of the USA, Australia sent land, air and sea forces to fight alongside the Americans in Vietnam. Mirroring the American experience, it was a painful era of bitter divisions on the home front.

A Cosmopolitan Country

Another obvious change in orientation is the racial and national background of Australians. Before World War II, almost the entire population was British born or of British descent. After the war, throngs of Greeks, Yugoslavs, Italians

and northern Europeans settled in Australia with more than 10 percent of immigrants refugees or displaced persons. The Asian presence today, swelled by more than 100,000 Vietnamese 'boat people' and other South-East Asian refugees, has begun to reflect the strength of trade ties with Australia's neighbours. Ambitious school children even study Japanese.

Even before the 'White Australia' policy was finally discarded in 1972, the official attitude towards the Aborigines had also softened. In 1960, the descendants of the original Australians were at last granted citizenship and social service benefits. While the Aborigines struggled for land rights, the government intensified efforts to overcome their disadvantages in health, wealth and education, but with few visible results. The Abo-

*P*olitical graffitti and fantasy art add colour to an already vibrant city.

rigines stopped calling themselves Aborigines, and used regional terms instead such as *Koorie*, *Nungga* and *Nyunga*.

In 1988 Australia celebrated 200 years of white settlement, in the face of Aboriginal protests. Queen Elizabeth II was on hand for the dedication of Sydney's biggest bicentennial project, Darling Harbour (see p.35). When the Queen returned in 1992 she was confronted by a vociferous movement calling for Australia to go it alone as a Republic.

In the 1980s and into the 90s, international and domestic economic difficulties darkened the abiding Australian dream of boundless prosperity. Unfinished and unoccupied skyscrapers troubled many Australian cities, and unemployment topped 10 percent. But with more than two centuries of pioneering spirit behind them, Australians place their bets on the Asian connection, and on natural resources like sunshine and friendly charm that point to a likely snowballing success in the phenomenon of tourism. **25**

Where to Go

Like Australia itself, Sydney sprawls so relentlessly that you must concede you'll probably never see it all. Don't despair. Many of the really essential sights are grouped within walking distance of one of the world's most dramatic harbours. The walkability is a distinct advantage in this city of slow-moving traffic, confusing signposting and chronic parking problems. Ferry boats, buses and trains serve non-walkable distances, as do taxis and water taxis.

To get some sort of perspective, admire the view from the top of Sydney's tallest buildings or take a helicopter tour. See the clear blue tentacles of water stretching from the South Pacific deep into the heart of the city. Schools of sailing boats, their colourful spinnakers puffed with pride, vaunt the harbour's perfection in the reflection of the sky-scrapers, the classic Harbour Bridge and the exhilarating Opera House. For another angle, see the city's skyline from sea level. Whether you decide to survey Australia's greatest harbour from the deck of a luxury liner, a sightseeing boat or a humble ferry, it's unforgettable.

To see Sydney close to, stroll through the delightful historic district of The Rocks, browse in the shopping centre, relax at Darling Harbour, explore the magnificent Opera House, and enjoy the local colour in the inner suburbs of lively King's Cross or trendy Paddington.

The Essentials

In a rush? Here are the principals not to be missed:

The Harbour: a dream setting

The Harbour Bridge: still looking good

The Opera House: a touch of class

The Rocks: history and distractions

Darling Harbour: mostly for fun

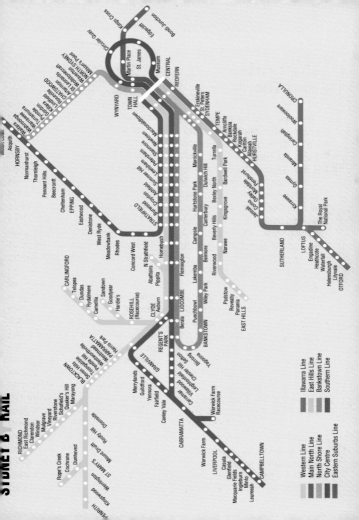

The Harbour and The Rocks

Governor Phillip and his First Fleet colonists would find it difficult to recognize Sydney Cove. Its modern name is **Circular Quay,** short for *Semi-*Circular Quay; in reality it's more rectangular. Most sightseeing tours – by land or sea – leave from Circular Quay. Cruise ships, sightseeing boats and water taxis tie up here, but most of the action involves everyday ferry boats and high-speed JetCats. Part of the attraction is the convergence of leisurely tourists, gawking at the sights, and harried commuters, who cross the harbour rarely glancing above the top of their newspapers at the splendour of it all. Adding to the non-stop hum of human interest are street musicians, mime artists and hawkers.

A leisurely 19th-century atmosphere spreads through **The Rocks**, the birthplace of the nation, overlooking the harbour. The calculated charm of the streets is perfect for

28

strolling, shopping, and stopping for a drink or meal. There are walking tours, or you can explore history in style from a horse-drawn carriage.

It was at The Rocks that the founding fathers came ashore in 1788 to build the colony of New South Wales. Restored and revivified, this historic waterfront district now offers stunning views, moody old buildings, and cheerful plazas. Wander at will or pick up local leaflets and maps at **The Rocks Visitors' Centre**, 104 George Street.

Next door, **The Story of Sydney** is one of those 'multi-dimensional experiences' designed to introduce the visitor to the local scene. It's a well-produced walk-through extravaganza of videos and special effects summarizing the often dramatic history of the city from Aboriginal times. On the way out, a small museum provides interesting footnotes to the story told through documents and artefacts, as well as reminders of some of the types of wildlife the pioneers found, starting with a stuffed dingo

W *here it all began, a ferry boat departing from Circular Quay is the best way to get a feel for the busy harbour.*

which emits howls recorded from a real version.

On the opposite side of The Rocks Visitors' Centre is **Cadman's Cottage**, Sydney's oldest surviving house (dating from 1816) – a simple stone cottage which was occupied for a long time by the government's boatsmen. John Cadman, a pardoned convict, was the original coxswain.

Before harbourside land was reclaimed, the water used to come right up to the house, in which you can view a small **29** collection of old anchors, sails and oars.

Campbell's Storehouse, further along the cove, is a venerable brick warehouse converted into an attractive complex of shops, restaurants and a wine bar. Another commercial highlight in a former warehouse, the **Argyle Arts Centre** is an early restoration project now housing restaurants, arts-and-crafts shops and interesting galleries.

WINNING MUSEUMS

A popular museum in The Rocks, **The Earth Exchange**, at 18 Hickson Road, cleverly enhances a geological exhibition with ecological messages. Expertly aimed at keeping the children interested, it provides 'hands-on' devices and fun interludes for everyone.

Definitely *not* a 'hands-on' part of the museum is the big, dramatically lit display of precious stones from all over Australia and the world. Ironically, the Jubilee Nugget, said to be 1½ million dollars worth of raw gold, must be the ugli-est item of them all, shaped like a huge human brain.

The **Museum of Contemporary Art** also gives new life to an old building, an Art Deco classic overlooking Circular Quay West. What other art museum in the world has such a view? The museum's benefactor, John Power, an Australian-born artist, died in obscurity in 1943. He left millions of dollars and about a thousand of his paintings, influenced by both Cubism and Surrealism, which make up the core of the collection. A further 3,000 or so come from artists as celebrated as Roy Lichtenstein, Robert Indiana, Gilbert and George, and Cindy Sherman. If they're too old hat for you, look for expositions from the most avant-garde. Almost any medium is valid here from painting to laser-generated art.

HISTORY IN THE MAKING

A look at **Argyle Cut**, a shady underpass, helps to understand why the first generation of convicts named this district The Rocks. To excavate this route, work parties in chains were ordered to hack through solid rock with pickaxes. It took years. In Sydney's boisterous 19th century, this was the likeliest place in town to be mugged.

High above The Rocks, **Observatory Hill** is a choice spot from which to observe Sydney Harbour. The hill, the summit of Sydney, has been the site of a windmill, a fort, a signal station and an astronomical observatory. Starting in the middle of the 19th century, at precisely 1pm every day, a ball was dropped from a mast here so ships' captains could set their chronometers. For a look at the stars of the southern sky, visit the **Museum of Astronomy**.

Groups of terraced houses on the Millers Point side of the peninsula are preserved as architectural monuments. So are a couple of the oldest pubs in Australia, redolent of history as well as beer. If you really need an excuse, the Hero of Waterloo in Lower Fort Street and the Lord Nelson Hotel near Argyle Place are worth visiting, if only for scholarly purposes.

For history without the refreshments, see the **Garrison Church**, officially called the Holy Trinity Anglican Church, which dates from the early 1840s. As the unofficial name indicates, it was the church for members of the garrison regiment, the men in charge of the convict colony. Sydney society today considers it a fashionable place to get married.

Back on the waterfront, **Pier One** is a former multi-storey shipping terminal now converted into a shopping and leisure centre with restaurants and views. From the grassy hillside of Dawes Point Park, studded with old cannons, you can survey the harbour's froth of ferries and JetCats.

THE BRIDGE

With its drive-through stone pillars and geometrically impeccable steel arch, **Sydney Harbour Bridge** strides confidently across the harbour. An impressive link joining the city to the North Shore, it is held in sentimental esteem.

It took nine years to build one of the foremost engineering achievements of the era. Before its construction the North Shore could only be reached by ferry. During the Great Depression of the 30s, Sydneysiders called the bridge the 'Iron Lung', for it kept many people 'breathing' – in economic terms. The span remains a steady source of employment for tollkeepers, daredevil painters and maintenance men. Repainting the entire bridge is a 10-year job, at which point it's time to start all over again.

Bridging the gap
To settle any bets, here are some vital Harbour Bridge statistics for the record:

The arch itself measures 503m (1,650ft), and carries eight lanes of cars, two railway tracks, plus lanes for pedestrians and cyclists. The top of the arch is as high above the harbour as a 40-storey building. Every year about 40 million vehicles pass over the landmark; during rush hour it may feel as if all 40 million are stalled on the approach roads.

Understandably nicknamed 'The Coathanger', the bridge was officially opened on 19 March 1932. To get a view of the bridge, the harbour and the city skyline, an unusual vantage point is the top of one of the bridge's massive pylons.

The lookout is in the south-east tower, and the stairway of 200 steps – if you can manage it – is reached via Cumberland Street, The Rocks. It is best, however, to confirm opening hours, so telephone 02/247 3408 in advance.

The City Centre

Skyscrapers are increasingly commonplace in Sydney, but at last count, **Sydney Tower** at Centrepoint still held the title of the city's highest vantage point at 305m (1,000ft), not to mention being the highest building in the Southern Hemisphere. It's open every day of the year except for Christmas Day. In only 40 seconds you whoosh straight up to the observation decks and revolving restaurants. Amateur photographers get that glazed look as they peer hungrily through the tinted windows to unlimited horizons. Fortunately there is also some *un*tinted glass so that cameras can capture authentic colours.

On a flawless day you can see all the way to Terrigal and Wollongong, or far out to sea or even to the Blue Mountains (see p.59). Close in, there's a new angle on the glory of the harbour and the precarious coexistence of Sydney's skyscrapers, highways and historic buildings.

Most Australian cities and towns now have pedestrian malls, normally at the heart of the downtown shopping district, lined with department stores and boutiques. Sydney's centre has a different sort of mall: **Martin Place** is a wide, pedestrian only street of trees, sculpture and fountains. It's just for strolling, meeting with friends, enjoying a takeaway lunch and breathing some non-air-conditioned air. At midday, free concerts are staged in a small amphitheatre, anything from rock to chamber music. The Cenotaph here is the goal of marchers taking part in April's Anzac Day Parade.

VICTORIANA

On the corner of Martin Place you can mail your postcards grandly from the imposing Victorian Renaissance building of the **General Post Office**. During World War II the GPO's clock tower was dismantled – not because the correct time was a military secret, but for fear Japanese bombers might zero in on the landmark. It wasn't put back again until more than twenty years later.

From the same era as the GPO, but even grander, the **Queen Victoria Building** occupies an entire block on George Street, Sydney's main street (and the oldest street in Australia). It began as a vast municipal market and commercial centre, including a hotel and a concert hall, and was topped by 21 domes. But business turned bad and in the bleak 1930s the city government converted it into offices and a library.

In the 1980s the building's fine stonework and interior details were restored to create a most appealing all-weather shopping centre. The QVB, as it is commonly known, houses close to 200 chic boutiques, plus cafés and restaurants, in a cool and unhurried atmosphere of calculated charm.

Next door, Sydney's **Town Hall** enlivens a site that used to be a cemetery. Compared with skyscrapers elsewhere in the area, this overblown Victorian building, begun in 1868,

*G*eorge Street has kept its elegant charm despite being one of the busiest shopping streets.

seems to be on its knees. But the clock tower, containing a two-ton bell, aims its cupola ostentatiously heavenward.

Home of the city council, this sumptuously appointed building is also used for exhibitions and concerts – indeed the 8,500-pipe organ is a monument in itself. **35**

Darling Harbour

Every Australian town built something new in honour of the Bicentennial observance of 1988, and Sydney's contribution was the nation's biggest urban redevelopment programme ever. The evolution of **Darling Harbour** from derelict seaside to a powerful pole of attraction for tourists and locals alike was accomplished in only four years.

Take the monorail from the central district of Sydney to this all-purpose leisure centre. The elevated track covers a 3½ km- (2 mile-) loop of six stations. Although it's gravely overcrowded at times, the monorail is mostly for fun. It may not be terribly practical, and many consider the pillars a blot on the city-scape, but it does serve as a useful vehicle for sightseeing. If you're anti-monorail, you can also walk there, take a shuttle bus or ferry boat from Circular Quay, or a water taxi. And if you have a car, don't worry – Darling Harbour is equipped with 6,000 parking spaces.

Shops covers gemstones and fancy fashions to the silliest souvenirs; you can never predict what the next one will offer. It's also well stocked with food outlets.

The **Australian National Maritime Museum** occupies a big, glass-walled building. The exhibits are divided into several themes: early explorers and what they found; the saga of the pioneers; the navy then and now; and how the seas serve the needs of commerce and recreation. Outside there are floating exhibits as varied as a century-old racing cutter, a battleship-grey destroyer, HMS *Vampire*, and a fragile Vietnamese fishing boat which was used to bring refugees to Australian shores in 1977.

SUPER-AQUARIUM

Across the historic **Pyrmont Bridge**, a drawbridge 30 years older than the Harbour Bridge, is an establishment self-proclaimed as the world's 'most spectacular aquarium'. At the **Sydney Aquarium**, start with the crocodiles, whose baleful immobility seems to challenge crowds to hang around until one of them stirs.

For children there is a 'touch pool' with sea urchins, abalone, anemone, shore crabs and other fascinating living creatures which can all be touched, gingerly, under the supervision of a friendly, knowledgeable guide. Micro-aquariums are equipped with remote controlled video cameras, which can zoom in on tiny exhibits.

But the most stirring experience is under sea level, where tourists are propelled through tunnels surrounded by sharks, graceful rayfish and other big game of the deep. Gazing at the wonders here is the next best thing to getting wet. Two oceanariums, devot-

The Rocks was the first sight the convicts had of Sydney. It looks a bit different now.

37

ed to deep-sea and Sydney harbour fish, contain a total of 2.75 million litres (605,000 gallons) of water. The astonishing sound effects you'll hear were recorded live.

At the inner end of Cockle Bay, the **Exhibition Centre** is designed on the suspension bridge principle, with cables attached to masts holding up the roofs. The glass walls of the exhibition halls look out on **Tumbalong Park** and the adjoining open spaces, more than just a pleasant place to soak up the sun. Here are brilliantly original fountains, geometrical challenges, swings, slides, and mazes, all ahead of conventional playgrounds.

SHOW BIZ

The **Sydney Entertainment Centre** predates the harbourside development. Designed for sports events, concerts and other public events, it can hold 12,500 spectators.

Next door, the **Pier Street Pumphouse**, a historic building, once supplied hydraulic pressure to operate lifts and the weighty doors of bank vaults. Restored, it serves the tourist thirst as a tavern.

Time out for meditation. Darling Harbour's Chinese Garden, officially called the Garden of Friendship, was a co-production of the governments of New South Wales

Chinatown

Unlike most Australian cities, Sydney's centre stays alive after dark. One focus of action is Chinatown, which keeps the lights on for gourmets. Estimated at about 60,000, the city's Chinese community shares its restaurants with enthusiastic Sydneysiders and tourists. The district's centrepiece is Dixon Street, a pedestrian zone framed by ceremonial wooden gates and illuminated by distinctive lamps. The cuisines of Peking, Canton and Szechuan form the backbone of the delights on offer, interspersed with shops selling exotic spices.

and the Chinese province of Guangdong. The one hectare (2½ acre) garden is packed full of appealing plants and trees such as apricot and azalea, jasmine and weeping willow. The paths, ponds and rock formations are designed to take you away from everyday life.

The good news about the **Powerhouse Museum** (by the monorail track at the southwest corner of Darling Harbour) starts at the entrance: admission is free. There is, in fact, nothing but good news to report about this museum. Australia's largest museum complex, it was once a powerhouse, generating electricity for the street trams. Essentially a science-and-industry museum, it is generously supplied with interactive attractions and houses thousands of exhibits, from an ancient steam locomotive to a Catalina flying boat, which hangs from one of the ceilings. There are also relics of space exploration, including samples of dehydrated food used by astronauts and cosmonauts. You can eat better at the museum's café.

Macquarie's Sydney

Almost in the shadow of the central district's skyscrapers, the Sydney that Governor Macquarie built is set among trees, grass and flowers. The parks are as historic as the buildings around them.

Although **Hyde Park** is only a fraction the size of its namesake in London, it provides the same green relief. The land was cleared at the beginning of the 19th century, with a race track as its first big attraction. Hyde Park was the chosen venue for boxing matches, and also the new colony's first cricket pitch. The most formal feature of these 16 ha (40 acres) of gardens, the **Anzac War Memorial**, commemorates the World War I fighters in monumental Art Deco style.

Sightseers who collect old churches should mark three targets on the edge of Hyde Park. To the north, the early colonial **St James's Church** in Queen's Square was the **39** work of the convict architect, Francis Greenway (see also p.42). Across College Street to the east, **St Mary's Cathedral** stands on the prominent site of the colony's first Catholic church, and from the same era, the magnificent **Great Synagogue** faces the park across Elizabeth Street.

The Anzac Day Parade and the War Memorial remember the dead from the First World War.

The welcome mat's out at the **Australian Museum**, on College Street, or so it says in nine languages as you enter. Inside is a survey of natural history, from fossils and dinosaurs to current ecological concerns. The stuffed birds – not to mention the bees, flies and spiders – are the sorts of 'educational' things schoolchildren are dragged to museums to be shown. But you can learn a lot about Australian animal life here. Another highlight is the section on the art, culture and recent history of the Aborigines. And take time to browse through the Aboriginal arts and crafts on sale in the Museum Shop.

Children are well catered for also in the restored **Hyde Park Barracks**, between the park and the Botanic Gardens. Designed by Francis Greenway in 1819 as the first respectable flop-house for ex-convicts, it is now a museum of social history. On the top floor of the barracks, one large room houses a complete reconstruction of the dormitory life of the prisoners.

*F*rancis Greenway, convict architect of the Hyde Park Barracks received a full pardon from Governor Macquarie on its opening.

The Mint, next door, has exhibits on money, stamps and flags. Here you can see the Holey Dollars – Spanish coins recycled to ease a desperate shortage of cash in New South Wales. The new colony used the equivalent of both the doughnut and the hole: the **41**

The Builder

Only in Australia would they put the portrait of a convict on the $10 note. And a forger, at that.

Francis Greenway was convicted of forging a clause in a building contract. In 1812 this crime carried the death penalty, but he was lucky: his sentence was commuted to 14 years exile in Australia. The dynamic Governor Lachlan Macquarie 'discovered' Greenway, the only competent builder in the colony, appointed him government architect and pardoned him. Greenway designed everything from churches to a lighthouse and his projects grew ever more dignified, to the delight of the Governor.

The bigwigs in London finally complained that extravagance had no place in a penal colony and Greenway was sacked in 1822, but his monuments are everywhere. If colonial Sydney had been ready for an Opera House, Greenway would have designed it.

---

centres were punched out and used as 15-pence coins, while the remaining outer rings became five-shilling coins, worth four times as much.

Continuing north along Macquarie Street (named after himself by the memorable, if immodest, governor), **Sydney Hospital** superseded the notorious Rum Hospital of the early colonial days. The **State Parliament House**, adjoining, has resounded to political debate, mostly sober, since the early days. The elegant houses opposite, among the city's most desirable, contain a high proportion of doctors' and lawyers' offices.

MORE THAN A PARK

The **State Library**, bordering the informal park called the Domain, is the ultimate trove holding documents on early explorations, the First Fleet and other historical themes. Classical columns announce the main portal of the Mitchell Wing, but next door, the nifty 1988 concrete and glass addition boosts the building's size and spirits. Amateur genealogists haunt this library, hoping to discover if their own ancestors were convicts or free men.

The Domain started as a private park for the governor, but for more than a century it has contained the Sydney version of London's Speaker's Corner (confusingly in Hyde Park in London!), where anyone can climb on a soapbox and hold forth; Sunday is the day of orators and hecklers. In January, during the Festival of Sydney, the Domain is the scene of open-air concerts.

Seven days a week art lovers come to the Domain to explore the **Art Gallery of New South Wales**. It consists of an old and newer building joined like ill-matched Siamese twins, plus a brilliant modern (1988) extension that adds both light and views of east Sydney and part of the harbour. The gallery provides a crash course in more than a century of traditional and modern Australian art. First-rate, too, is an Asian collection going back 3,000 years, and an enviable hoard of the sculptures and masks of South Pacific islanders. The concise review of Australian Aboriginal art – wood sculptures and paintings on bark and canvas – covers a lot of ground, both artistically and ethnologically. There are free guided tours and, when you need a break, an inviting café-restaurant.

An impressive building, the State Library houses a vast collection on Australia and the Pacific.

Sydney Opera House, one of the wonders of the modern world – stunning from any angle.

Sydney's **Royal Botanic Gardens** began as a different sort of garden, where the early settlers first attempted to grow vegetables. The First Fleet had picked up plants and seeds on the way to Australia, but no-one in the new colony seemed to have green fingers. Today, only a few steps away from the busy skyscraper world of downtown Sydney, you can relax in the tranquil shade of Moreton Bay fig trees, palms or mighty mahoganies, or enjoy a glass pyramid full of orchids and other tropical beauties. Birds of many species inhabit the trees, roam the lawns and take advantage of the fountains.

The gardens curve around Farm Cove up to a peninsula with the somewhat quaint name of **Mrs Macquarie's Point**. Thus immortalized, the **44** wife of the governor used to admire the view from here; nowadays it's better than ever.

THE OPERA HOUSE

Australia's best-known man-made symbol, a one-in-a-million building covered in a

million tiles, does the impossible: it embellishes a perfect harbour. In a country with a notoriously casual lifestyle, the **Sydney Opera House** conveys a sense of occasion. It's hard to imagine the harbour without it. It has brought glory to the city, the country, and the architect who left in a huff at an early stage in its construction (see p.46).

Until the 1950s, the promontory here was wasted on a fancy, turreted depot for tramcars – hardly a site for sore **45** eyes. Then the government of New South Wales decided to make the most of Bennelong Point and build an arts centre.

Hundreds of architects entered an international design competition, and the winner was a Dane, Jørn Utzon. His novel plan touched on problems of spherical geometry so complicated that he actually chopped up a wooden sphere to prove it could be done. The inspiring exterior of the building had virtually been completed when the melancholy Utzon, harried by officials and the trade unions, walked out in 1966. The interior plan subsequently became the work of a committee of four Australian architects.

Despite this, the finished product has grace, taste and class from the tip of its highest roof, 67m (221ft) above sea level, to the Drama Theatre's orchestra pit, situated more than a fathom *below* sea level.

It's too late to change it now, but the name Sydney Opera House is, strictly speaking, inaccurate. The opera theatre itself is only one of the five halls, and not the biggest. It's well worth taking one of

High Finance

'Cost overruns' are a common problem on big construction projects, but the Sydney Opera House is a classic in its own right. At the outset, the budget stood at $7 million. By the time it was finished 19 years later, the price had zoomed to more than $100 million. The problem was solved in a typically Australian way, however: culture-lovers and others bought special lottery tickets which more than paid the bill.

Those ingenious billowing roofs, looking light as air, weigh 160,965 tonnes. Covering the roofs are 1,056,000 Swedish ceramic tiles which wash themselves when it rains. There are 6,223 sq m (66,595 sq ft) of glass, made in France. The biggest of the five theatres, the Concert Hall, seats 2,690 people.

the hour-long guided tours around the whole premises. They depart every 15 minutes from 9am to 4pm.

KING'S CROSS

If you're looking for the bright lights, take one of the reliable forms of public transport to the rakish excitement of The Cross. X marks the spot for X-rated entertainment and re-creation. In Queen Victoria's day, King's Cross was known as Queen's Cross, but if Victoria came to visit now, she would not be amused.

Just east of the niftily named district of Woolloo-mooloo, loose-moraled King's Cross is Sydney's answer to Paris's Pigalle or London's Soho. By night it's electric, sleazy and fun, crawling with hedonists of all persuasions. Everything is for sale. Door-men importune almost all the passers-by, and so, less push-ily, do hordes of streetwalkers. Fortune tellers, drug vendors, artisans and eccentrics of just about every type complete the rich cast of characters.

This gaudy nightlife dis-trict has more to offer, how-ever, than mere sin. There are reputable hotels and shops and good ethnic restaurants.

A five-minute walk from King's Cross Station, **Eliza-beth Bay House** is a magnifi-cent stately home built in 1835 for the colonial secretary in the style of a Grecian villa. It has now been restored, filled with period furniture and is open for inspection (except on Mondays). Beyond the classi-cally inspired porch, the centre of architectural interest is an ingenious elliptical staircase, suitable for even the most dramatic entrance.

BOHEMIAN `PADDO'

Another inner suburb worth investigating is **Paddington**, to the south east of King's Cross. Its trademark is intri-cate wrought-ironwork, com-monly known as Sydney Lace, which you'll see adorning the balconies of many of the 19th-century terraced houses.

This frilly feature, and the rather bohemian atmosphere, **47** reminds some travellers of New Orleans. After decades of dilapidation, the district has become a fashionable, rather arty place to live. 'Paddo' as the locals like to call it, is full of interesting places to live in, unusual ethnic restaurants, antique shops, art galleries and trendy boutiques.

The **Victoria Barracks**, along Oxford Street, is a formidable example of mid-19th-century military architecture. It was built by convicts, far from what was at that time the centre of Sydney, to house a regiment of British soldiers and their families. At 10am every Tuesday (except during December and January) a formal changing of the guard ceremony, marching band and all, is held at the barracks. Afterwards, visitors can take a tour of the establishment. And it's all free.

South of these barracks, **Centennial Park** has been a breath of fresh air for city folk since 1888. Adjoining its 220 hectares (544 acres) of trees, lawns, duck ponds, rose gardens and bridle-paths is Moore

Park, the famous Sydney Cricket Ground (a landmark to fans from all over the world), the Sydney Football Stadium and the Royal Showgrounds.

Harbour Isles

Sydney Harbour is more complex than it first appears, but a couple of ferry rides will help to sort out some of the ins and outs. Or you can hire a boat of your own. Better yet, avoid the nautical traffic problems and join the cheery throng aboard one of the many sightseeing cruises departing from Circular Quay. The commentary is usually amusing and enlightening, and you'll discover hidden beaches, mansions old and new, islets, and even a couple of unsung bridges.

For your first foray across the harbour, try the ferry ride going from Circular Quay to **Taronga Zoo.** This is where most foreign tourists experience their first meeting with kangaroos and koalas. The setting can't be beaten: over the heads of the giraffes you can

48

*T*he sometimes comical looking sulphur-crested cockatoo is well known throughout Australia.

look across the harbour to the skyscrapers of central Sydney. Taronga Zoo houses a particularly chirpy collection of 1,500 Australian birds of about 200 species. As for the indigenous animals, they're all on view, including night creatures illuminated in artificial moonlight. See the only platypus in town, swimming in his big fishbowl. The dozing koalas are rallied for a photo opportunity from 1 to 2pm; around 3pm, they reawaken for their food. If you arrange your visit around feeding times, which are posted at the gate, you can watch the keepers distribute food while they deliver talks about their charges.

Fort Denison occupies a small harbour island known as 'Pinchgut'. In the early days, it served as a prison island. Considering that at the time the whole of Australia was a prison island, it must have been pretty bad here. Indeed, troublesome convicts endured a bread-and-water diet, which accounts for Pinchgut's nickname. A rare, and embarrassing attack on Fort Denison came in World War II when a stray shell from an American warship nicked the top of Old Pinchgut's martello tower. To tour the island, sign up for a cruise from Circular Quay; advance booking is essential.

A stately home with its own beach, **Vaucluse House** adds its mock-Gothic turrets to the skyline. The mansion began as the home of a colourful convict, Sir Henry Brown Hayes, the sheriff of Cork be-

The kangaroo got its name after Captain Cook asked an Aboriginal to tell him what the strange marsupial was called. It turned out later that the word kangaroo is a native expression for 'I don't know'.

fore he was banished to Australia for the abduction of his bride. In the 1830s the new owner, William Wentworth, expanded it into a 15-room homestead which is now run by the Historic Houses Trust.

The Beaches

Dozens of inviting beaches offering raging surf or inviting waves stretch both north and south of Sydney. They are as essential a part of Sydney life as the backyard barbecue. In summer you must swim only between the life-guard flags.

BONDI BEACH

Pronounced 'bond-eye', this is the closest beach to central Sydney, a distinction assuring it a packed house on summer weekends. A complete range of facilities, from showers to cafés, provides all comforts, except solitude. The varied cast of characters on the sand includes ancient sunworshippers, bathing beauties and fanatical surfers. If a warning bell clangs, it's not the end of a lifeguard shift but a shark alert, which it is best to take seriously although sharks are less of a problem than some other marine life.

SOUTH FROM BONDI

Among the most beautiful of the beaches in greater Sydney, **Tamarama** is noted for topless sunbathing. Not good for families as the waves can get very rough. **Bronte**, backed by palms and Norfolk pines, has plenty of facilities. **Coogee** beach is better than most for swimming and **Cronulla**, to the south of Botany Bay, is vast, not crowded, and usually of interest to surfers.

BOTANY BAY

Captain Cook's landing place is bypassed by the excursion coaches and beyond the range of public buses and trains. It's about 30 km (18 miles) by car from the central business district to Kurnell, where the National Parks Service runs a museum celebrating the 1770 visit of Cook and his eager botanists. Lining a path in the park beyond the museum, there are monuments and markers to point out details such as the stream from which the *Endeavour* took on fresh water and the burial place of the first European to die in Australia. The park is alive with Australian magpies and flashy lorikeets, just the sort of exhibits that the pioneering botanist Joseph Banks would have loved to catalogue.

NORTH OF SYDNEY

Manly got its name, the story goes, because the first governor of the colony thought that the Aborigines sunning themselves on the beach looked manly. A ferry boat or hydro-

*B*ondi, Sydney's most famous beach – perfect for surf and sun – an Australian love affair.

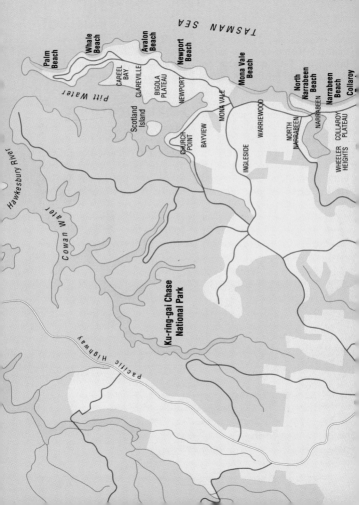

TASMAN SEA

Palm
Beach

Whale
Beach

Avalon
Beach

Newport
Beach

Mona Vale
Beach

North
Narrabeen
Beach

Narrabeen
Beach

Collaroy

CAREEL
BAY

CLAREVILLE

BIGOLA
PLATEAU

NEWPORT

Scotland
Island

Pitt Water

MONA VALE

WARRIEWOOD

NORTH
NARRABEEN

NARRABEEN

COLLAROY
PLATEAU

WHEELER
HEIGHTS

CHURCH
POINT

BAYVIEW

INGLESIDE

Hawkesbury River

Cowan Water

Ku-ring-gai Chase
National Park

Pacific Highway

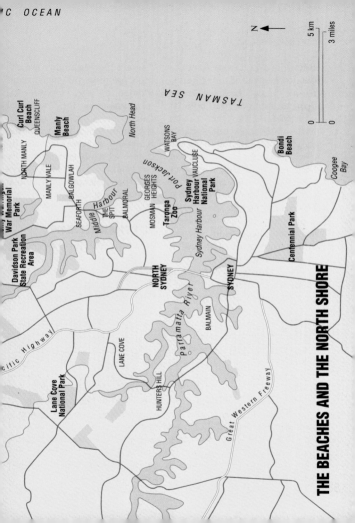

foil ride away from Circular Quay, cheerful Manly offers a choice of two beaches – one open to the ocean and popular with surfers, the other a calm harbourside crescent suitable for children. Linking them, the lively Corso is a pleasant Mediterranean-style promenade which is lined with restaurants, fast-food emporia, ice-cream stands and souvenirs. For decades the resort has used the slogan, 'Seven miles from Sydney – and a thousand miles from care.'

The **Manly Oceanarium** claims to have Australia's largest collection of marine life. Among the highlights are the high-jumping fur seals. Supplementing the conventional viewing tanks, the Tunnel of Life offers a thrilling perspective on undersea life: a moving walkway traverses an acrylic tunnel which is surrounded by freely swimming sharks, rays and their friends. Quite close enough for comfort.

FURTHER NORTH

North of Manly, a couple of Pacific beaches with charming names are **Curl Curl** and **Dee-Why**, both good for surfing. **Collaroy** and **Narrabeen** are

---

Life Savers

Surf bathing didn't strike Australia's fancy until the beginning of the 20th century. Only a wave or two later, the first life-guards plunged in, and the Bondi Beach Life Saving Club was founded in 1906.

Armed with rope reels or rescue boards and boats, the highly trained life-savers in their colourful bathing caps are a reassuring part of Australia's ocean scen-ery. Around the coastline they have saved hundreds of thousands of swimmers in trouble.

Two changes have come about in recent times: professional life-guards now work alongside the volunteers, and women are welcomed into the corps.

To defend local modesty, bathing during daylight hours was banned at Manly until 1903.

linked by a single super beach, ideal for families and with an ocean pool. **Newport Beach** is a beautiful, broad beach. **Avalon Beach** is good for surfing and popular with children. At the northern tip of the Sydney beach region, **Palm Beach** is in a class of its own. The hills of the peninsula behind Palm Beach are occupied by manicured, nicely gardened villas and the view from the lighthouse is well worth the climb. **57**

Day Trips

By now you're ready to venture beyond Sydney to the Australia of your preconceptions – to the bush and the strangely tinted land of gum and wattles, the sort of scenery in which a leaping kangaroo wouldn't look at all out of place. In the vastness of New South Wales you can find all this and more – deserts and rainforest included.

Even within day trip distance of Sydney, you can feast your eyes on scenery memorable for its beauty or its eccentricity. The most popular northern destination is the Hunter Valley, a picturesque winegrowing region. To the south lie stunning seascapes, heartwarming landscapes and historic towns; excursion firms

Parramatta Farmers

Parramatta, about 25 km (15 miles) west of the central business district, claims many 'firsts' in Australian history: first market place, woollen mill, vineyard, observatory, and an important achievement: the first legal brewery.

Lucky James Ruse, who claimed to have been the first man ashore when the First Fleet landed, may well have been the only convict with any farming experience. As the colony was desperate for food, the governor granted him a 16-ha (40-acre) spread in Parramatta, which was candidly called Experiment Farm. Ruse provided the hungry colony's first wheat crop.

A farmer of quite a different style, John Macarthur, arrived as a young officer with the Second Fleet. He named his 40-ha (100-acre) Parramatta estate Elizabeth Farm, after his wife. Their house, now 'the oldest existing house in Australia', was a well-designed three-room cottage. Much expanded over the years, it's quite stately today, with lovely gardens. Like Experiment Farm Cottage and several other historic sites in Parramatta, it's open for visits.

even run day trips to Canberra and back (see p.76). Further west, the big attractions are the inspiring Blue Mountains and Jenolan Caves.

Blue Mountains

Beyond Parramatta, perhaps the most extraordinary sight in all of New South Wales is the hazy spectacle of the **Blue Mountains**. The blueness is attributed to the refraction of light through the haze of eucalyptus oil evaporating from the billions of leaves.

Botanists, geologists, ornithologists and even just plain tourists rave about this rugged range which hems in metropolitan Sydney. They seemed insurmountable to early explorers who tried to get across by following the valleys, but discovered the deep gorges to be daunting and impassable. The solution came when, in 1813, a party of explorers – Blaxland, Lawson and Wentworth – finally conquered the obstacle by crossing the summits (see also p.19).

Sun-bleached bark – a common sight in a country where the blistering heat can be relentless.

The Blue Mountains are an escape from Sydney's summer heat, a chance to inhale the cool, fragrant air and listen to the birds. The communications network is so good that some Sydneysiders now live here and commute to work: trains link Sydney's Central Station **59** and the region's tourist centre, **Katoomba**. The 19th-century town (its name means 'falling water') looks out over a well-known rock formation, the **Three Sisters**.

The inevitable legend that shrouds the sculptured outcrop goes like this: the three sisters were turned to stone by their witch doctor father in order to save them from the jaws of the dreaded bunyip whom they had accidentally awakened. The father changed himself into a lyrebird and hid in a cave, but lost his magic bone in the process. He is still looking for it today, and while the three sisters watch and wait on their mountain ledge, you can hear the call of Tyawan the lyrebird echoing through the valley.

Everywhere you go, there are delightful bushwalks along clifftops or valley floor, and basalt and sandstone cliffs to please even the most discerning mountain-climber. Exciting perspectives on all this are offered from the Scenic Railway (originally used to haul coal), claiming to be the world's steepest railway line, with an incline ratio of more than 1 in 2. For an equally exciting excursion across the gorges, take the Scenic Skyway, a cable car dangling high above the valley.

JENOLAN CAVES

A thrillingly steep drive down the mountains from Katoomba leads to Australia's most famous underground attraction, the **Jenolan Caves.** For more than a century, spelunkers and ordinary tourists have admired the stalactites, stalagmites and special effects, but explorers have yet to penetrate the entire labyrinth. The caves first came to public attention in 1838, when a lawman tracking down a fugitive (who was using them as a hideout) stumbled on the entrance.

Guided tours through the spooky but often awesome limestone caverns last about an hour and a half. The atmosphere is cool in summer, warm in winter, and always somewhat damp, just the way you'd expect a cave to be.

*P*eaceful, verdant landcapes away from the hustle of Sydney. No wonder some have chosen to live here and commute to the city. **61**

Hunter Valley

The famous wines of the **Hunter Valley** go back to the earliest days of Australian history. The young colony's first vines, planted in Sydney, had come a cropper because of the rocky soil, the climate and the salt air. In a new experiment, cuttings from vineyards in France and Spain were planted in these rolling hills that start about 100 km (60 miles) north of Sydney. By the middle of the 19th century, the region was producing hundreds of thousands of bottles per year. Nowadays Australia accounts for something like one per cent of all the world's wine – more than enough to keep the country in good spirits; the overflow is exported.

Wine-tasters start their researches in the district's main town, **Cessnock**, 195 km (120 miles) north of Sydney, which is surrounded by about 30 wineries. Many of these offer tastings, but the 'cellar doors' can be jam packed on weekends and holidays. To discourage flightier visitors, most of the wineries now charge an entry fee. But you're under no obligation to buy.

At night the infernal fires of the steelworks announce **Newcastle**, the biggest city in the Hunter Valley. This centre of coal-mining and heavy in-

Soles to Newcastle

If you like long walks, the path from Sydney to Newcastle – more than 160 km (about 100 miles) – has everything from cityscapes to rainforest.

The Great North Walk, as it's called, begins in the suburb of Hunters Hill. The route soon leaves behind the pace of the city and goes bush. To rest tired feet, a ferry boat crosses the Hawkesbury River starting from Brooklyn. After Brisbane Waters National Park you're almost halfway there. Less dedicated hikers skip some of the stages by hopping on public transport.

dustry has recently put the emphasis on tourism and high-tech industries. It's strong on parks and beaches, including a superb surfing beach. In the spacious seaport, a drab warehouse zone has been replaced by the sprawling A$13-million Queen's Wharf leisure development (where you'll find the tourist office). On a promontory overlooking the harbour, big guns still testify to an historic incident of World War II. Fort Scratchley was the only naval artillery battery in Australia to have fired in anger. The target was an attacking Japanese submarine, which quickly fled. If you're in cultural mood, head for the Newcastle Regional Art Gallery, home of some admirable modern Australian paintings.

LAKE MACQUARIE

South of Newcastle, and continuing the city's aquatic playground theme, is Australia's largest saltwater lake. **Lake Macquarie** is popular with weekend fishermen and sailors who like a good yacht race without having to risk their lives in the Pacific. In fact, sailing regattas have been held here regularly for more than a century.

Hawkesbury

Australia is not particularly well endowed with rivers: many of them peter out after the wet season. Dependably navigable, though, is the **Hawkesbury River**, which winds along for 480 km (about 300 miles) on its way to the Pacific at Broken Bay, just beyond Palm Beach. Boatsmen rave about its sparkling waters and ever-changing vistas – coves and bays and steep wooded banks. One unusual way of experiencing the river is to travel aboard the mail boat, which maintains the postal lifeline. It sets off every morning from Monday to Friday and also on Wednesday and Friday afternoons from the quay at Brooklyn.

Wiseman's Ferry has been a port since 1817, when an enterprising former convict, **63**

Headgear at Old Sydney Town – not much change today from the colony's first 20 years.

Solomon Wiseman, opened an inn and started ferrying cattle and people across the river. **Dharug National Park**, on the far shore, is a mostly unspoiled domain of cliffs and gullies, rich in wild flowers, inviting bushwalks, picnic and camping areas. There are ancient Aboriginal sites, and by way of more recent history you can walk along part of the Old Great North Road, built by chain gangs in the 1820s.

North of the Hawkesbury, at Gosford, the atmosphere of the original penal colony has been recreated at **Old Sydney Town**. Budding local actors in period costume duel, march, fire muskets, and re-enact situations to amuse and inform visitors of all ages. A blacksmith, a potter and a candlestick-maker work at their craft, and a 'magistrate' shows the way summary justice used to be delivered.

On the way to Old Sydney Town, the Pacific Highway takes you through **Ku-ring-gai Chase National Park**. Definitely worth a detour, this area of unspoiled forests, cliffs and heathland is home to numerous species of animals and 160 varieties of bird. But you must find them for yourself; it's not a zoo. By way of man-made attractions, the Aborigines, who lived in this area long before the foundation of New South Wales, left hundreds of rock carvings of animals and supernatural beings. The park information centre has maps pinpointing the location of the most interesting carvings. From the information centre, a 15-minute orientation walk has been laid out; it's easy enough to do with a baby buggy or a wheelchair.

A Selection of Hotels and Restaurants in Sydney

Recommended Hotels

To help you choose a hotel, the following list is a selection based on price, attraction and location. Included are Sydney, Canberra, and other towns in New South Wales.

The hotels range from luxurious to moderately priced to more spartan accommodation. The following price guide applies for a double room:

III+ high international standard (from A$240 upwards in Sydney, from A$150 upwards in smaller cities)

III expensive (from A$120-240 in Sydney, from A$100-150 elsewhere)

II moderate (about A$70-120 in Sydney, A$60-100 elsewhere)

I less than A$70 in Sydney, less than A$60 elsewhere)

Backpackers hostels (of which there are plenty, particularly in the King's Cross area) are not listed here, but start at about A$10 per night.

SYDNEY

Astoria |
9 Darlinghurst Road, King's Cross
Tel. 02/356 3666
Budget accommodation in lively King's Cross.

Coronation |
7 Park Street
Tel. 02/267 8362
Cheap and cheerful. Round the corner from the Town Hall.

Crest Hotel III
111 Darlinghurst Road, King's Cross
Tel. 02/358 2755
A 15-storey hotel overlooking swinging King's Cross.

Hilton International III+
259 Pitt Street
Tel. 02/266 0610
At the monorail station, a very central international-class skyscraper hotel, recently renovated to a very high standard.

Holiday Inn Menzies   ▓▓▓+

14 Carrington Street
Tel. 02/299 1000
Traditional favourite with 441 spacious rooms, four restaurants, pool and spa.

Hotel Nikko Darling Harbour   ▓▓▓+

161 Sussex Street
Tel. 02/299 1231
Australia's largest hotel, this 649-room establishment overlooks the stunning new development of Darling Harbour. There's a Japanese department store on the premises.

Hyatt Kingsgate   ▓▓▓+

Corner Victoria Street and King's Cross Road, King's Cross
Tel. 02/356 1234
33-storey landmark in exciting King's Cross.

Hyde Park Inn   ▓▓▓

271 Elizabeth Street
Tel. 02/264 6001
Comfortable 15-storey motel overlooking Hyde Park.

Inter-Continental   ▓▓▓+

117 Macquarie Street
Tel. 02/230 0200
A large, smart, modern hotel inhabiting the historic shell of the 1851 Treasury Building.

Macquarie Hotel   ▓▓

Corner Hughes Street and Tusculum Street, Pott's Point
Tel. 02/358 4122
Small and old-fashioned hotel socking any guests who smoke with a 10% surcharge.

The Manhattan   ▓▓

8 Greenknowe Avenue, Pott's Point
Tel. 02/358 1288
Comfortable accommodation between Elizabeth Bay and King's Cross.

Oxford Koala Hotel   ▓▓▓

Corner Oxford Street and Pelican Street
Tel. 02/269 0645
Big, popular motel just south east of Hyde Park.

Oxford Towers Motor Inn   ▓▓

13 Waine Street, Darlinghurst
Tel. 02/267 8066
Within walking distance of the city centre.

Park Hyatt   ▓▓▓+

7 Hickson Road, The Rocks
Tel. 02/241 1234
Understated, intimate, low-rise luxury, beautifully set on the waterfront. A butler tends to each floor and there are two phone lines in each room.

67

Park Regis   ‖

Corner Castlereagh Street and Park Street
Tel. 02/267 6511
Reasonably priced and comfortable accommodation between the Town Hall and Hyde Park.

Ramada Renaissance   ‖‖+

30 Pitt Street
Tel. 02/259 7000
Lavish version of 'European elegance' with 562 rooms. Harbour and city views.

The Regent Sydney   ‖‖+

199 George Street
Tel. 02/238 0000
Nearly 600 rooms in this refurbished harbourfront winner commanding The Rocks. A very popular choice for tourists.

The Russell   ‖

George Street
Tel. 02/241 3543
Small and friendly establishment in The Rocks, full of character.

Sheraton Wentworth   ‖‖+

61 Phillip Street
Tel. 02/230 0700
In the heart of the busy financial district, this grand hotel has more than 400 delightfully refurbished rooms and a ballroom.

CANBERRA

Canberra City Motor Inn   ‖‖

Corner Northbourne Avenue and Cooyong Street
Tel. 06/249 6911
72 units, swimming pool.

Capital Parkroyal   ‖‖+

1 Binara Street
Tel. 06/247 8999
Canberra's biggest hotel, part of the National Convention Centre.

Crest Motor Inn   ‖

60 Crawford Street, Queanbeyan
Tel. 06/297 1677
25 budget-priced rooms a short drive from Canberra.

Embassy   ‖‖

Hopetoun Circuit and Adelaide Avenue, Deakin
Tel. 06/281 1322
In the diplomatic area, one km (½ mile) from Parliament House.

The Hyatt Hotel Canberra   ‖‖+

Commonwealth Avenue, Yarralumla
Tel. 06/270 1234
Elegant restored 1920s charm.

Lakeside   ‖‖

London Circuit
Tel. 06/247 6244

On the shore of Lake Burley Griffin with a 15th-floor restaurant.

CESSNOCK, NSW

Cessnock Motel ▮▮
13 Allandale Road
Tel. 049/90 2699
20 units, centrally located.

Hunter Valley Motel ▮▮
30 Allandale Road
Tel. 049/90 1722
Comfortable and friendly. Closest motel to the vineyards.

GOULBURN, NSW

Centretown Lagoon ▮▮
77 Lagoon Street
Tel. 048/21 2422
40-unit motel, indoor pool.

Posthouse Motor Lodge ▮▮
1 Lagoon Street
Tel. 048/21 5666
38-unit motel, outdoor pool.

KATOOMBA, NSW

Echo Point Motor Inn ▮
Echo Point Road
Tel. 047/82 2088
Near the lookout point.

Katoomba Town Centre ▮▮
224 Katoomba Street
Tel. 047/82 1266
Comfort in the heart of town.

NEW CASTLE, NSW

Newcastle Ambassador ▮▮▮
King Street and Steel Street
Tel. 049/26 3777
6-storey motel right in the centre of town.

Noah's On The Beach ▮▮▮
Shortland Esplanade and Zaara Street
Tel. 049/29 5181
Magnificent views overlooking the South Pacific.

PARRAMATTA, NSW

Parramatta City ▮▮
Corner Great Western Highway and Marsden Street
Tel. 02/635 7266
Views over Parramatta Park.

Parramatta Parkroyal ▮▮▮+
30 Phillip Street
Tel. 02/689 3333
Parramatta's first international class hotel, 12 storeys high.

69

Recommended Restaurants

Sydney has a vast and multinational range of restaurants and eating places. The following is a selection of restaurants recommended by recent travellers. If you find other places worthy of recommendation, we'd be pleased to hear from you.

To give you some idea of prices, the following symbols denote the average cost of a three-course meal for one (without wine):

	in Sydney	elsewhere
▌▌▌	above A$60	above A$35
▌▌	A$35-60	A$25-35
▌	below A$35	below A$25

SYDNEY

The Art Gallery Restaurant ▌
Art Gallery of NSW, Mezzanine Level, Art Gallery Road
Tel. 02/232 5425
Australian cuisine and wines. Lunch only, Sunday-Friday.

The Bathers Pavilion ▌▌
The Esplanade, Balmoral Beach
Tel. 02/968 1133
Fabulous ocean view to complement outstanding seafood dishes.

Bennelong ▌▌
Sydney Opera House, Circular Quay
Tel. 02/250 7578
A theatrically sumptuous setting before or after the opera.

Berowra Waters Inn ▌▌▌
Berowra Waters
Tel. 02/456 1027
Nouvelle cuisine, panoramic view.

Bilson's ▌▌
Circular Quay West
Tel. 02/251 5600
Views of the Harbour and Opera House. Inventive French cuisine.

China Sea ▌
94 Hay Street, Haymarket
Tel. 02/211 1698
Authentic Chinese restaurant in the bustling heart of Chinatown.

Diethnes Greek Restaurant ▌
336 Pitt Street
Tel. 02/267 8956

Old World atmosphere in which to sample moussaka, lamb and Greek-style seafood.

Doyles

11 Marine Parade, Watson's Bay
Tel. 02/337 2007
On the beach – an old tradition. Very big and popular. Every kind of seafood imaginable.

Fine Bouche

191 Palmer Street, East Sydney
Tel. 02/331 4821
Highly regarded *haute cuisine* in informal surroundings.

Imperial Peking Harbourside

15 Circular Quay West, The Rocks
Tel. 02/277 0736
Although far from Chinatown, all the traditional Chinese delights, especially seafood.

Jordon's

197 Harbourside, Darling Harbour
Tel. 02/281 3711
Right on the harbour. Seafood specialities, plus outdoor dining and music.

Last Aussie Fishcaf

24 Bayswater Road, King's Cross
Tel. 02/356 2911
Fish and chips, char-grilled octopus. Music, dancing.

Oasis Seros

495 Oxford Street, Paddington
Tel. 02/33 3377
Gourmet delights in romantic ambience with fireplaces in winter. Ambitious, original cuisine.

Phantom Of The Opera

17/21 Circular Quay West, The Rocks
Tel. 02/247 2755
Strong on seafood dishes. Glorious view. Outdoor dining.

Rockpool

109 George Street, The Rocks
Tel. 02/252 1888
First-class atmosphere, food and service. Seafood fantasies under Asian influences.

Siam

383 Oxford Street, Paddington
Tel. 02/331 2669
Spicy Thai delights.

Suntory

529 Kent Street
Tel. 02/267 2900
Sushi, *sashimi* and fine Japanese cuisine using the freshest seafood.

The Wharf Restaurant

Pier 4, Hickson Road, Walsh Bay
Tel. 02/247 9245
Varied Australian cuisine, with harbour view.

71

CANBERRA

Comme Chez Soi
Ginninderra Village, Barton Highway
Tel. 06/30 2657
Belgian cuisine, of all things, in a very Australian atmosphere.

Fringe Benefits
54 Marcus Clarke Street
Tel. 06/247 4042
Luxury meets *haute cuisine* at this friendly brasserie.

Le Gourmet
4 Colby Court, Philip
Tel. 06/82 3363
French cuisine in elegant surroundings.

Imperial Court
40 Northbourne Avenue
Tel 06/48 5547
Elegant atmosphere for tasty Cantonese cooking.

Innovations Restaurant
35 Kennedy Street, Kingston
Tel. 06/95 7377
Australian food as authentic as wichetty grubs. Lavish decor.

Mama's Trattoria
Garema Place
Tel. 06/48 0936
Italian family-style pasta.

Mirrabook Restaurant
Australian National Gallery
Tel. 06/273 2836
Lunch with a view of the lake.

Terminus Tavern
9 East Row, Civic
Tel. 06/49 6990
Do-it-yourself barbecues.

KURRAJONG HEIGHTS, NSW

Patrick's Pressoir
Kurrajong Heights
Tel. 045/67 7295
Haute cuisine with a view overlooking the Hawkesbury Valley.

POKOLBIN, NSW

Pokolbin Cellar
Hungerford Hill Wine Village, Pokolbin
Tel. 049/98 7584
Delightful atmosphere – perfect for Hunter Valley explorers.

WOLLONGONG, NSW

Harbour Front Restaurant
Endeavour Drive, Wollongong
Tel. 042/27 2999
Good view. Seafood specialities.

Animal Life

Within day trip distance of Sydney, many private parks cater to visitors who'd like to get to know the native animals at closer range. Some visits are on organised excursion itineraries. Below we list a selection of wildlife and similar parks (not in any particular order of merit, but alphabetically).

Australian Reptile Park, near Gosford. Lovely alligators, crocodiles, pythons and cobras waiting to greet you. If you're not keen on fondling a lizard or watching the handler milking a venomous snake, you can concentrate on more cuddly exhibits, like koalas and kangaroos.

Australian Wildlife Park, one hour's drive west of central Sydney in Eastern Creek, has kangaroos as tame as your cat, but friendlier. If the koalas are unenthusiastic about posing for pictures, it may be because they are nocturnal creatures and would frankly rather be asleep.

Australia's Wonderland, beside the Australian Wildlife Park (at Minchinbury, near Blacktown), is a very large amusement park with water slides and one of the world's biggest wooden roller coasters. A busy day for kids.

The Bounders

Kangaroos come in all sizes, from the red – often taller than a man – to the musk kangaroo, no taller than a year-old child. With their deer-like faces and congenial personalities, kangaroos can be very appealing, though not to farmers whose grain they appropriate.

The joey, born in an embryonic stage, moves into the mother's pouch for about six months of nursing. Kangaroos can freeze the chain of reproduction in time of drought or disaster, putting an embryo in limbo until conditions improve. Thus their race prospers... in leaps and bounds.

73

Koala Park Sanctuary, at West Pennant Hills, between Parramatta and Hornsby, was founded in 1930. The adorable koalas do little but eat and sleep, yawn, sigh and scratch themselves. Kangaroos wait to be petted and brilliantly coloured native birds hang out in roomy aviaries.

Tobruk Merino Sheep Station, near Wiseman's Ferry, is a working sheep station. Personable experts explain all aspects of the processes of raising sheep, rounding them up, shearing them, sorting the wool and packing it for export. Tourists also get to try their hand, usually with hilarious results, at shearing.

Waratah Park, 35 minutes from downtown Sydney on the edge of Ku-ring-gai Chase National Park. Koalas available for petting, and gregarious kangaroos, too. Waratah Park was the location for the television series *Skippy the Bush Kangaroo*.

Further Afield

Southern Highlands

Linking Australia's two biggest cities, Sydney and Melbourne, the Hume Highway traverses the Southern Highlands – lush grazing land and orchards interrupted by towns and villages straight out of the history books.

The Victorian era comes first, with the 'gateway to the Southern Highlands', **Mittagong**. In the middle of the 19th century this was an iron-smelting town. Among the tourist attractions here today, you can lose yourself in the gargantuan maze, or commune with fluttering flocks of lepidopterous delights in the Butterfly House. A short 5 km (3 miles) south, **Bowral** is a

Colonial reminders are dotted about Bowral, a main town in the Southern Highlands.

prettily gardened town with a tulip festival every October. It used to be a favourite resort for Sydney's upper crust.

The Hume Highway slices through charming **Berrima**, a Georgian gem so precious that the whole town is listed as a national monument. There is no shortage of antique shops, arts-and-crafts galleries and atmospheric tea shops. Among the many distinguished monuments, the **Surveyor General Inn**, established 1834, claims to be Australia's oldest continuously licensed inn and makes an appealingly historic spot for a drink or a meal. Another landmark, the **Berrima Gaol**, was built by its inhabitants in the 1830s.

Bundanoon was the honeymoon haven for Sydney-siders a couple of generations before the discovery of cheap flights to Bali. The highland climate and vegetation suggest an affinity with Scotland, and a Gaelic-style festival is held every April. The town sits on the edge of **Morton National Park**, noted for its gorges and gullies, and suitable for either **75**

peaceful strolls or rigorous bushwallks. A moving highlight is **Fitzroy Falls** which cascade 82m (269ft) from a sandstone cliff.

Canberra

The Australian (artificial) capital, set in the wilderness for political reasons, is vast and green and impossible to get around without a car.

This city's story goes back to the turn of the 20th century. As the new Commonwealth was proclaimed, the perennial power struggle between Sydney and Melbourne reached an awkward deadlock. To invent a model capital from scratch, Australia opened an international competition. The prize went to an American architect, Walter Burley Griffin, but it took longer than anyone imagined to convert his grand plan into reality (owing to the distractions of two world wars, the Depression, and a great deal of wrangling) and sadly Griffin, a Chicagoan of the Frank Lloyd Wright school of

architecture, died in 1937 before Canberra was established as the political capital.

At the heart of the state known as the Australian Capital Territory (ACT), Canberra has a population of 280,000 and is essentially a one-company town; the government's. The ministries are here, as well as parliament with its politicians, lobbyists and foreign embassies.

Pedestrians are out of luck in the great expanses of this city of parks, which is further complicated by a network of crescents, curving roads and circles that would baffle Christopher Columbus. It's a good idea to sign up for a bus tour; they come in half-day and all-day versions, or take the Explorer bus, which stops at all the main sights. Motorists can pick up a sightseeing pamphlet at the Visitor Information Centre, Northbourne Avenue, Dickson. The Canberra Visitor Centre can be found in the Jolimont Centre, Northbourne Avenue, Dickson.

An effective starting place for a do-it-yourself tour is

Regatta Point, overlooking the lake that Burley Griffin cleverly surrounded with a city. The **Canberra Planning Exhibition** uses three-dimensional mock-ups and audiovisual techniques to sum up the capital from its beginnings into the future.

Lake Burley Griffin, 35 km (22 miles) in circumference, is named after the town planner who realized the value of water for recreation as well as scenic beauty. Board a sightseeing cruise boat, or look into the fishing, sailing and windsurfing possibilities. Foaming up from the lake, a giant **water jet** honours the explorer Captain Cook for several hours each day, a refreshing sight in summer. The **Carillon**, another monument rising from Lake Burley Griffin (actually from a small island), was presented as a gift from the British government. The music emanating from its 53 bells, the biggest weighing six tons, can comfortably be heard within a radius of 300m (980ft). Apart from concert recitals, it tells the time every 15 minutes.

Canberra's 'provisional' Parliament House, a building of understated dignity, served as the seat of government for more than 60 years. A belated replacement, now the permanent **Parliament House**, was dedicated by Queen Elizabeth

---

Meeting Place

Canberra's name is derived from an Aboriginal word meaning meeting place. It was officially chosen in 1913 from an outpouring of suggestions, some as uplifting as 'Utopia' or 'Shakespeare'. Other proposals were inventions like 'Auralia' and 'Austropolis'.

The most unusual nomination was a wild coinage designed to satisfy the ambitions of every state capital that lost out in the running for federal power – Sydmeladperbrisho. Compared with that mouthful, the name Canberra sounds like pure poetry.

II in the bicentennial year of 1988. Its trademark is a four-legged stainless steel flagpole which stretches 81m (265ft) above the roof.

The combination of unusual design and exploding building costs rendered the new complex on Capital Hill a billion-dollar *cause célèbre*. Taxpayers were quick to note the lavish offices, bars, swimming pool and sauna. But the politicians were prudent enough to include plenty of facilities for the public – galleries for witnessing the debates, exhibitions, and a cafeteria.

To get the full impressive picture, take in Canberra from the top of the **Telecom Tower** on Black Mountain. Millions have ascended this dynamic tower 195m (640ft) high for its 360° panoramic views. Thanks to Canberra's pollution-free atmosphere, it's worthwhile, even at night, when the public buildings are illuminated.

On the eastern slopes of Black Mountain, the **National Botanic Gardens** are devoted to Australian plant life – the most comprehensive collec-tion anywhere on earth. You can inspect more than 6,000 species of native plant, including hundreds of varieties of eucalyptus (favourite with the koala). Nature trails are marked among the 40 ha (100 acres) of forests and gardens.

The original business and shopping district of the **Civic Centre** was opened in 1927 (ancient history by Canberra's standards) with symmetrical white colonnaded buildings in a mock-Spanish style. Nearby are shopping malls and the Canberra Theatre Centre.

One of Canberra's most famous and interesting landmarks, the **Australian Academy of Science**, is for looking and photographing but unfortunately not for visiting. The stunning, low slung copper-plated dome rests on graceful arches standing in a circular moat. Some say it looks like a flying saucer at rest.

The Australian War Memorial – one of the most visited sights in the nation.

A more conventional dome covers the vast and impressive **Australian War Memorial**, a sandstone shrine at the end of Anzac Parade. You"ll find that there are war memorials all over Australia, but this is the definitive one, drawing around a million visitors a year. It's hard not to be swept up in the mood as you walk past walls inscribed with the names of more than 100,000 of Australia's war dead.

Beyond the heroic statues and mosaic murals, the memorial is also a museum, with displays of uniforms through the years, plus battle maps, and plenty of hardware ranging from rifles and battle tanks up to an actual World War II Lancaster bomber.

The **Australian National Gallery** shows artists as varied as Monet and Matisse, Jackson Pollock and Willem de Kooning, and also an honour roll of Australian masters. A high point is the collection of original Australian Aboriginal art.

In the south-west district of Deakin, the **Royal Australian Mint** punches out the nation's coins. The factory also 'moonlights' to produce the coins of several other countries. The Mint's own museum contains coins and medals of special value. If it's hundred dollar notes that attract you, you've come to the wrong fortress: all the paper money is printed in Melbourne.

The **National Science and Technology Centre** is an exemplary model of a new

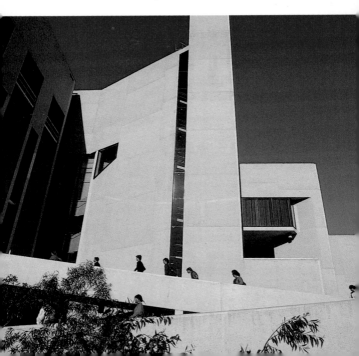

generation of museums jam packed with interactive hands-on exhibits. They simulate 55 earthquakes a day (6.9 on the Richter scale), plus other experiences involving gravity, lightning and other dramatic natural phenomena.

In the early days, diplomats dreaded the prospect of being transferred to the wilderness of Canberra, and most countries dragged their feet about moving their **embassies** until Prime Minister Menzies got tough in the 1950s. The **US Embassy** is a perfect replica of an 18th-century American mansion, the Thai Embassy boasts sweeping roofs and the Indonesian Embassy is decorated with statues of legendary figures. The Japanese Embassy even has a tea house in its formal garden.

Australian wildlife is on view at the **Tidbinbilla Nature Reserve**, 40 km (25 miles) south west of Canberra. It has thousands of acres of bushland where native animals and plants flourish. Kangaroo fans can feed the bounders in a reserve within the reserve. The walking trails are graded from easy to exhausting.

North Coast

Endless beaches, accessible rainforest, and plenty of activities keep surfers and sun-bathers from all over the state and beyond coming back to the resorts of the North Coast of New South Wales, alias the Holiday Coast.

Half-way up the coast from Sydney to the Queensland border, the resort centre of **Port Macquarie** claims its climate is the best anywhere. If so, you may well ask, why was it chosen, in 1821, as the site of a penal colony within a penal colony? Why punish the more troublesome convicts in such agreeable surroundings? The catch was its inaccessibility, but that minor problem was soon solved as roads were **81**

The Australian National Gallery, one of the capital's dynamic modern structures.

built, and free settlers swarmed in. Find out more about the early days of colonial life in the award-winning **Hastings District Historical Museum**. History buffs will also want to visit **St Thomas' Church**, built by convicts in 1824. In addition to the beaches and all manner of watersports, the area is also rich in commercial tourist attractions like koala parks, dolphin shows and children's amusements.

Inland from Port Macquarie, **Timbertown** is an interesting working reconstruction of a 19th-century village and its logging operation. Covering over 35 hectares (86 acres), this prominent tourist attraction brings back to life several aspects of the lumber industry, from the clang of the village blacksmith to the screech of a steam-powered sawmill.

Northwards, **Coff's Harbour** has miles of beaches. Fishing boats and pleasure craft occupy the harbour, and the shore is exceptionally well supplied with good shops, restaurants and nightspots. Just north of the town, you can't miss one of Australia's pioneering efforts in more kitsch gigantism, the **Big Banana**, a walk-through tribute to a local delicacy.

Banana splits, cakes and every other variation of the fruit imaginable are sold on the garish premises, now expanded into a horticultural theme park.

Sleepy Lagoon

The jurisdiction of New South Wales juts far into the South Pacific. The outpost of Lord Howe Island, some 480 km (300 miles) east of Port Macquarie, is the world's most southerly coral isle, providing splendid snorkelling and scuba diving. On land are fascinating plants and birds, most remarkably the local woodhen, which can't fly. Lord Howe Island is almost car free, but anyway, even if you insist on taking your car, the speed limit is 25 kph (15 mph).

The coast road north from Coff's Harbour to **Byron Bay** is a thriller. A brave lighthouse blinks the news that Cape Byron is Australasia's easternmost point. The perfect setting (a hang-gliding favourite), and the supply of underpopulated beaches, attracts artists and surfers, not to mention humpback whales which can be spotted offshore every winter.

South Coast

Leaving Sydney, the southbound (Route 1) Princes Highway skirts the airport and the suburbs before revealing the beautiful wilderness of **Royal National Park.** This is the world's second oldest national park – after Yellowstone Park in the USA – and, best of all, it's only 36 km (22 miles) from the big city. Hiking trails crisscross the park's 15,000 hectares (37,000 acres), which lead to both swimming and boating spots and some impressive waterfalls.

South of it, Highway 1 is strictly businesslike, but if you choose the coast road, you'll experience more invigorating scenery. At the appropriately named **Sublime Point**, 415m (1,360ft) above sea level, there is a marvellous ocean view. The same scenery can be admired from a different viewpoint, a few hundred metres south at **Bulli Lookout**.

From here, too, you can see the smokestacks of **Wollongong**, New South Wales' third largest city. Beaches and a pleasant fishing port nearby soften the industrial profile of blast furnaces and factories. Wollongong also has a prizewinning pedestrian mall with 400 shops.

Beyond the salt lake, **Lake Illawarra**, a popular recreation area, is a famous natural phenomenon – the **blowhole** at **Kiama**. When the ocean is in fierce mood, the explosion of sea water is a sight – and sound – to remember. In fact it's so rousing that floodlights have been installed.

Beyond the commercial fishing port and tourist centre of Ulladulla, beautiful, oyster-rich **Bateman's Bay** was **83** named by Captain Cook in 1770. Nestling at the foot of the Clyde Mountain Ranges, it's the closest seaside resort to Canberra.

Big-game fishermen delight in **Narooma**. From here the boats head for Montague Island, where marlin, kingfish and yellowfin tuna are to be found, among others. Luckier are the penguins and seals, for whom the island is preserved as a sanctuary.

The delightful fishing port of **Bermagui** was little known until Zane Grey, the American writer of cowboy stories, visited in the 1930s and reported on the hefty marlin he caught. Good game fishing and opportunities for all kinds of watersports can be found along the Sapphire Coast, so dubbed because of the colour of the sea in these parts.

The most southerly port in New South Wales, the old whaling town of **Eden**, commands spectacular Twofold Bay, known as the world's third deepest natural harbour. Notwithstanding its virtues, Eden is named after a 19th-century British statesman, not Adam and Eve's garden.

Canberra at Sea

Landlocked Canberra enjoys a pretty toehold in the South Pacific, thanks to some inspired gerrymandering. **Jervis Bay**, a New South Wales peninsula south of Nowra, was annexed to the Australian Capital Territory early in the 20th century. The enclave today includes an uncommon combination of facilities: the Royal Australian Naval College, a missile range, inviting dunes and beaches, and a nature reserve.

See the wreck of the Cape St George lighthouse. This 19th-century beacon was built in the wrong place, invisible to northbound ships. Worse, the construction itself was considered a hazard to navigation. The navy took aim and reduced it to a historic ruin.

SNOWY MOUNTAINS

The top of the world – or at least the top of Australia – is in the south-eastern corner of New South Wales. The Snowy Mountains aren't going to put the winter resorts of the Rockies or the Alps out of business, but they are usually skiable in July, August and September, and there's certainly less competition then. Even during the summer a few drifts of snow remain to frame the wild flowers of the Australian Alps. The summit is Mount Kosciusko, 2,228m (7,316ft), named after an 18th-century Polish patriot by a 19th-century Polish explorer. It is the source of three important rivers, the Murray, Murrumbidgee and Snowy.

Kosciusko National Park is about 6,300 sq km (2,450 sq miles) of a combination of flora that you won't see anywhere else: buttercups, bluebells, eucalyptus and snow. The only missing element is the pines. Cars must be fitted with snow chains from 1 June to 10 October. But even in summer, when the bushwalks are delightful, the weather can take a rapid change for the worse, so you should carry a warm, waterproof jacket.

The first to ski here were gold rush fortune-hunters of the 1860s, who improvised at cross-country with the most elementary equipment. Nowadays several resorts of a certain sophistication cater to both downhill and cross-country skiers. The best known, **Thredbo Village** (with the steepest slopes) and **Perisher Valley**, have plenty of accommodation, ski-lifts, and après-ski facilities.

Westward Ho!

Explorers, chain-gangs, pioneers and gold prospectors led the way beyond the Great Dividing Range into the central west region of New South Wales. The route to take is the Great Western Highway, which was opened in the early 19th century by highly motivated pioneers, including convicts who built the road in exchange for pardons. **85**

The industrial and coal-mining city of **Lithgow**, 140 km (87 miles) west of Sydney, has the Lithgow Valley Zig-zag Railway, tortuously linking mountain with valley, and one of the wonders of engineering exploits during the Victorian era. Tunnel-building progress made it redundant in 1910, but the original route was so remarkable, and the views so glorious, that part of the itinerary has been revived for vintage steam fans.

Australia's oldest inland city, **Bathurst**, was founded in 1815 by Governor Macquarie himself. Among the many historic buildings is the Victorian Renaissance courthouse in a gardened setting facing King's Parade. The tourist office and a historical museum occupy the east wing. You won't be in Bathurst long before you hear about the city's favourite son, Ben Chifley (1885-1951), an engine driver who went on to be active in trade unions and politics, and from 1945-49 held the job of Prime Minister of Australia. Pilgrims come from all over to visit his humble family home in Busby Street, South Bathurst.

The agricultural region around the old town of **Mudgee** flourishes with cattle-graz-

*B*urning wastes of barren soil
– The Outback poet Henry Lawson knew his subject.

ing and crops ranging from wheat to wine. There are about 20 wineries in the area, most of them still family-owned and hospitable. Honey is another valuable product to come from these green valleys, with opportunities for more tastings for the discerning palate.

In the gold rush days, when the footlights were up at the Prince of Wales Opera House, the local boosters used to call **Gulgong** the 'Athens of the West'. If you suspect hyperbole, consider that the population in bonanza times was ten times bigger than today. Around the town, 170 buildings are classified as historically significant, with hitching posts and drinking troughs for

horses still in place. The bush poet Henry Lawson grew up in Gulgong; he and the town were immortalized on the back of the Australian $10 note.

In the spacious city of **Dubbo**, founded in the 1840s, is the Old Gaol, meticulously restored – the gallows had a last fling in 1904. Just out of town, the Western Plains Zoo, Australia's first open-range zoo, is a cageless convention of koalas, dingos and emus, plus more outlandish animals (at least to Australians) like giraffes, zebras and monkeys.

The Outback

There's nothing like it: red desert, ghost towns, stunted eucalyptus trees, and people vastly outnumbered by sheep and kangaroos. Within New South Wales, the most populous and productive state in Australia, you can travel to the real Australian Outback – bushland and cattle stations that seem far more than a thousand miles from comfortable **88** commuterland.

Lightning Ridge, set in stark, desolate country near the Queensland border, bears one of the most evocative of Outback names. Within a couple of miles of the town are several opal mines where you can learn all about precious black opals, and buy some if you wish. Anywhere else in this Back of Beyond landscape, proceed with caution – first so you don't fall into a hole, and second so you can't be suspected of trying to pillage somebody's stake. Some areas have been set aside for tourists who wish to try their hand at fossicking.

Bourke looks a lot bigger on the map than on the ground. 'Back of Bourke' is an Australian expression for really far out Outback. It's best to stay away in midsummer, when the temperature has been known to top 50°C (122°F) in the shade. Any other time, soak up the ambience in this old river port outpost.

Legendary for its mineral wealth, **Broken Hill** (population more than 25,000) is about as far west as you can go in New South Wales and is almost on the border with South Australia. Millions of tons of silver, lead and zinc ore are extracted from here every year. You can visit the mines, and there are mining museums and exhibitions of minerals and relics from the pioneering days.

The neatly laid out town, its streets named after minerals – Iodide, Kaolin, Talc – is something of an artistic centre as well, with works by acclaimed Outback painters on show in local galleries. At Broken Hill airport you can visit the Royal Flying Doctor Service, where they'll brief you on emergency healthcare in the Outback. Or for some really offbeat sightseeing, join the pilot of the mail plane that serves about 30 remote farms on its nine-hour circuit.

Silverton, a veritable ghost town 25 km (15 miles) west of Broken Hill, looks almost too good to be true. But it's an authentic restoration of the original mining town (one-time population 3,000), with the obligatory jail as its key historic monument, along with a couple of Victorian churches and a former brothel. Dozens of films have been shot here, including *A Town Like Alice* and *Mad Max 2*.

Beastly Flies

In the Outback, waving your hand in front of your face becomes second nature, like a horse flicking its tail. 'The Great Australian Salute', as the involuntary gesture is wryly known, aims to disperse the aggressive bush flies. The little buzzers harass people because they're thirsty and hope to lap up some moisture from human perspiration, saliva, or tears. Aside from hand signals, you might try wearing one of those silly hats with bobbing corks. The good news: scientists report there are fewer flies in the bush these days, thanks to colonies of African dung beetles unleashed to devour the insects' food sources.

89

What to Do

Shopping

Sydney shopping hours run from 9am to 5.30pm, Monday to Friday, and Saturday until 5pm. Shops do not close for lunch or at any other point during the day. Thursday is late shopping night, when many stores stay open until 9pm. (Darling Harbour shops stay open until 9pm daily).

Duty-free shopping is very competitive and highly organized, and not just at the airport. Japanese made stereos and cameras, as well as the more familiar perfumes and spirits, have particularly appealing price tags. You have to produce your air ticket and passport at the duty-free store when making your purchase and remember not to open the packages before you leave the country. On your departure you have to show them to the customs agent. Tipped off by the computer, he'll be looking out for you.

WHERE TO SHOP

In Sydney, skyscrapers sit above subterranean shopping arcades, and the Pitt Street Mall is linked to several shopping plazas. The centre's principal pedestrian plaza, Martin Place, is not a shopping mall at all but a perfect place to relax in between sorties. For shopping in a historic atmosphere, try the Queen Victoria Building, the Strand Arcade or the Imperial Arcade. A fashionable new shopping mall, Sky Garden, has upmarket boutiques in a spacious modern atmosphere, with restaurants on the glass-roofed top floor. If you're mobile, you'll find some of the suburbs have shopping complexes complete with acres of parking space. At the beach, the sun might inflate the price but the swimwear and leisure fashions will match your mood.

The Strand Arcade – a classic elegant landmark with fine cast-iron lacework and stained glass.

WHAT TO BUY

The temptations are as diverse as tacky knick-knacks to true works of art.

Aboriginal arts

Outback artists produce traditional paintings on bark, the subjects and styles recalling the prehistoric rock paintings: look out for kangaroos, emus, snakes, crocodiles, and impressions of tribal ceremonies. Craftsmen also produce decorated wooden shields and, inevitably, boomerangs. Better boomerangs, hand carved and painted, can reach quite expensive heights.

Antiques

Some worthy colonial pieces are furniture, clocks, jewellery, porcelain, silverware, glassware, books and maps. The Paddington district is full of antique shops.

Diamonds

In sheer volume, Australia outsparkles the world's other diamond producers. Look out in particular for the cut-and-polished results – precious stones in yellow, brown or white, but especially pink.

Fashions

Australian fashion designers get high marks for their relaxed, sometimes eccentric

Flea Markets

Brilliant with local colour, flea markets are a fine opportunity to mingle with the people and – who knows? – perhaps find something to buy: modern hand-painted pottery or home-made jam or a garden gnome. Saturdays are the time. Some of the places: **Paddington Village Bazaar** (Oxford and Newcombe Streets, Paddington) for original crafts, including avant-garde items, and second-hand goods. **Balmain Markets** (Darling and Curtis Streets, Balmain) for antiques and less expensive second-hand items. **Paddy's Market** (next to Redford Railway Station – Sundays too) for souvenirs, semi-antiques, and a wonderful array of foods.

styles and rousing colours. Swimwear, shorts and T-shirts (now a revered item of clothing thanks to colourful, popular designs by the well-known artist Ken Done) are likely to excite admiration back home.

Opals

Australia produces the great majority of the world's opals. Coober Pedy, in South Australia, the continent's biggest opal field, provides the white, or milky, opal. In the Outback of Queensland, around Quilpie, the reward is the 'boulder' opal, with brilliant colours and patterns. Lightning Ridge in New South Wales is the source of black opals (more blue than black) – the most expensive of all. Considered among Australia's best buys, opals are sold unset or as finished jewellery. The bigger jewellery shops can arrange tax-free purchases for foreign visitors, but you'll have to pay duty when you arrive home.

Outback clothing

You don't have to leave Sydney to buy a bit of ruggedness. Flannel shirts, moleskin (a durable form of cotton)

Genuine Aboriginal arts make interesting gifts, but paintings can reach four figures.

trousers, kangaroo-hide belts, and oilskin coats ('drizabones' – so named because that's what they keep you in heavy rain). You may take a shine to those cowboy-style hats that protect the cattlemen from sun and rain. Or go home in a digger hat, the comical-looking kind with a chin-strap and one side of the brim up.

Sheepskin

With Australian sheep outnumbering people by maybe ten to one, it's no surprise that sheepskin products are widely available, and usually at good prices. You can buy sheepskin

Sports

Every country has its sports fans, but Australia's are truly fanatics – not just enthusiasts, but frenzied compulsives. When they're not playing or watching sport, the Aussies are reading about it, arguing about it or betting on it.

WATERSPORTS

Swimming

Naturally, swimming is a major attraction with dozens of alluring beaches within easy reach of Sydney. But whatever your stroke, the surf can be as dangerous as it is invigorating. The more popular beaches are delineated by flags showing where it's safe to bathe. Beware of undertow or shifting currents and always obey the instructions of lifeguards, who aren't just there to flex their muscles. Sharks are a real, everyday problem; when a shark alert is sounded, beat a retreat to the shore and ask questions later. In spite of their mild name, jellyfish are a serious seasonal danger – it is

boots, hats, coats, rugs, toys, wall-hangings – you name it.

Souvenirs

Ingenious, inventive or hackneyed, souvenirs tend to pop up everywhere. The top sellers are miniature kangaroos and koalas, with plastic boomerangs not far behind.

95

The First Fleet came by sail – and they've been sailing in the perfect harbour here ever since.

Scuba diving

The best place in Australia for scuba diving – quite possibly the best place in the world – is the coral wonderland of the Great Barrier Reef. Sydney divers go down under at North Head. For information on the scuba scene in New South Wales, telephone the Australian Underwater Federation, 02/529 6496.

Surfing

Surfing areas are marked by signs, flags or discs. The best-known surfing zone in the whole of Australia is Bondi Beach. Manly is another favourite, and there are many other choice locations up and down the coast of New South Wales and beyond. Spectacular surfing carnivals are just some of the highlights of the Sydney season from November to March .

Sailboarding (windsurfing)

The brilliantly-hued sails add to the spectacle of the harbour as they whizz past many a cove. The sport is also very popular on lakes and rivers which are within day trip distance of the city.

best to check before you put a foot in the surf. And a final cautionary reminder: the sun is more powerful than you think. Apply sunscreen to exposed skin, wear a hat or try to stay out of the midday sun.

Boating

Sydney's prime yacht clubs are the Royal Sydney and the Cruising Yacht Club. Sailing boats and powerboats can be chartered, with or without a professional skipper. Inland, you can command a sailing boat on one of the lakes or a houseboat on the relaxing Murray River. Or you might just settle for an hour's hire of a pedalboat.

Fishing

For information about deep-sea expeditions from Sydney, check with the Sydney Game Fishing Club, Watsons Bay, telephone 02/337 5687. For outstanding trout fishing, try the icy rivers of the Snowy Mountains; details from the NSW Travel Centre, telephone 02/231 4444.

SPORTS ASHORE

Football

Several different kinds of football (commonly referred to throughout the country as 'footy') are played. Rugby Union, with teams of 15, is fast, rough and engrossing to the fans. Rugby League, the professional, international version, is the main event in Sydney. It's a rough-house game offering tough physical challenges to the players, 13 to a side. Australian Rules Football combines elements of rugby and Gaelic football. Look for long-distance kicks and passes and high scoring on an over-

---

Phar from the Madding Crowd

Only a sports-crazed country could enthrone a racehorse as a national hero.

Phar Lap, winner by three lengths of the 1930 Melbourne Cup, having survived a couple of assassination attempts, died in mysterious circumstances after a heroic victory in the United States; flags flew at half mast in Sydney. Today the taxidermist's version of him, under glass, is the star attraction in Melbourne's National Museum, and his mighty heart is preserved in the Institute of Anatomy in Canberra.

97

sized but overpopulated field – with 18 players to a side.

Golf

Golf clubs frequently operate under exchange agreements with clubs overseas, or you may have to be introduced by a local member. Alternatively, you can play on one of the public courses, of which there are dozens within the Sydney area. Check the New South Wales Golf Association, telephone 02/-264 8433.

Tennis

Whether the scene is Wimbledon, Flushing Meadow or the Australian Open, Aussie tennis players have always won more than their share of the championships. You'll find no shortage of courts, or partners in Sydney. The NSW Tennis Asociation can provide details; telephone 02/331 4144.

Skiing

The downhill season in the Australian Alps usually lasts from June until September, and sometimes into November, which should be inducement enough for skiers from the northern hemisphere. Some of the best-known and best-equipped resorts in the New South Wales Snowy Mountains include Thredbo Village (see p.85), Perisher Valley and Smiggin Holes.

SPECTATOR SPORTS

Cricket

They've been playing cricket since the early days of the penal colony at Sydney Cove. Purists deplore recent innovations, devised in Australia.

In its classical, white flannel form, the game would go on interminably. Kerry Packer, the well-known billionaire, established World Series cricket in 1977, with teams decked out in gaudy, colourful uniforms playing at night under the lights. Shockingly, too, they end the match decisively in a single day. Old die hard fans, however, can still follow the old-fashioned Test matches as well, every summer in Sydney.

Horse-racing

In Australia, horse-racing is closely entwined with local life. Nearly every town, even in The Outback, has a race track, and Sydney has four: Canterbury, Randwick, Rosehill and Warwick Farm; every Saturday of the year one of them is operating. Betting on horses, and almost anything else that moves, is as Australian as an ice-cold tinny.

Entertainment

The abundance of Sydney's racy entertainment should not be in the least bit shocking to anyone familiar with Australia's lusty history. What may come as a surprise is the richness of cultural attractions in a country not famous for its subtlety: opera, ballet, concerts, drama. Between the highbrow and the mindlessly relaxing, there will be something for all who just want an evening on the town.

THEATRE

Drama is lively, with professional companies producing the classics, recent British or American hits, and locally written plays. The big musi-

cals are staged at theatres like Her Majesty's or the Theatre Royal. Reservations for most theatres and concerts can be made by telephone: Ticketek, 02/266 4800. Or try your luck at the Halftix booth in Martin Place, which sells cut-rate tickets for the same evening's performances, though not for all shows. It operates from noon to 6pm Monday to Saturday; cash only.

Hall of Fame

Many an Australian has made the world headlines in sports. Some of their names are part of history:

Tennis: Ken Rosewall, Lew Hoad, Evonne Goolagong, John Newcombe, Pat Cash, Rod Laver, Margaret Court.

Golf: Jim Ferrier, Peter Thompson, David Graham, Greg Norman.

Swimming: John Marshall, Dawn Fraser, Shane Gould.

Cricket: Don Bradman, Ian and Greg Chappell, Dennis Lillee, Rodney Marsh.

MUSIC

Opera

Although you don't have to dress up, seeing grand opera in the Sydney Opera House turns the occasion into something even more sumptuous. The Australian Opera, the country's biggest performing arts company, is based in the Sydney Opera House.

Ballet

The Australian Ballet, founded in 1962, has its headquarters in Melbourne but spends nearly half its time performing in Sydney. Among the foremost modern dance troupes are the Sydney Dance Company and the Australian Dance Theatre.

Concerts

The concert hall of the Sydney Opera House, Town Hall and the Conservatorium of Music are the main venues for serious music. There is also a steady stream of good recorded music on ABC-FM radio.

Jazz and Pop

Sydney has an outstanding jazz menu which encompasses all the trends, traditional and avant-garde, mellow and raucous. In big or intimate jazz clubs, you might hear a visiting immortal or an up-and-coming local band. Clubs, cafés, pubs and taverns all over are filled with sounds from bush ballads to flashy new pop groups following in the footsteps of such luminaries as Olivia Newton-John, Rick Springfield, AC/DC, the Bee Gees, and INXS.

NIGHTLIFE

Sydney doesn't dim the lights after dinner. Nightlife flourishes in an array of conventional nightclubs, discotheques (trendy and otherwise – check the fashions), cocktail lounges, music pubs and karaoke bars. Just about every species of naughty activity can be found in the King's Cross district, which seethes with forbidden pleasures far into the night.

Incidentally, Sydney is the only state capital which does not have a gambling casino. In other cities and resorts in Australia it is legal to spend the night playing roulette, craps and blackjack.

CINEMA

Multi-screen cinemas are still going strong in Sydney, mostly along George Street. There are also specialized cinemas for art films, foreign films and revivals. The latest Hollywood releases hit the Sydney cinemas not long after their release in America.

The Australian film industry has been a major contributor to the art of moving pictures. Some of the big ones of modern times – *Picnic at Hanging Rock*, *My Brilliant Career*, *Breaker Morant*, the *Mad Max* series, *Gallipoli*, *The Year of Living Dangerously*, and *Crocodile Dundee* – have given the world a look at Australia's scenery as well as an insight into the national character and preoccupations.

CALENDAR OF EVENTS

January
Festival of Sydney.
Manly Summer Festival.
Australia Day (26 January).
February
Sydney Gay Mardi Gras Australasian Country Music Festival.
March-April
Royal Easter Show, Moore Park.
ANZAC Day Parade (25 April).
Sydney Garden Show.
May
Sydney Jazz Week.
Sydney to Brisbane Yacht Race.
June
Manly Food and Wine Festival.
Sydney Film Festival.
July
International Boat Show.
Blue Mountains: Yulefest.
August
City to Surf Fun Run.
Newcastle: Jazz Festival.
September
Australian Open Tennis Championships.
October
Bathurst: 1000 Motor Race.
Manly Jazz Festival.
Hunter Valley: Wine Festival.
November
Horse of the Year Show.
December
Sydney to Hobart Yacht Race (starts 26 December).

Eating Out

Sydney's 2,000 or more restaurants probably offer more than your appetite can deal with. They come in all styles, from internationally elegant establishments to neighbourhood bistros where you bring your own wine.

Serious food-lovers, who care less about candlelight and stylish service than the quality of the cuisine, may need to be reassured. All those clichés about a dreary diet of meat, potatoes and beer are as outdated as pounds, shillings and pence. Australians really care about what they eat nowadays and sophistication has been firmly installed. Some of the country's top chefs have plunged into deep eclectic waters. It's adventurous dining.

Even the simplest fare is based on wholesome ingredients. Thanks both to the generous climate and the abundance of grazing land, oceans and farms, there is a year-round supply of lean beef, lamb, fresh seafood and vegetables.

The wealth of the ocean – prawns, scallops, oysters, – tastes even better when you're eating it beside the harbour.

What's Cooking

To start with, people are of two minds about breakfast. Some can face the day with only a pastry and coffee, while in the restaurants of big hotels you may be greeted with a whopping buffet of fruit, eggs, meats and breads. Many a café will rustle up a hearty Australian breakfast with steak and eggs, lamb chops and eggs, and baked beans on toast. Can lunch be far behind?

FISH AND SEAFOOD

Oceans temperate and tropical provide a generous, varied catch of fish and seafood. If all you want is fish and chips

Outside dining is the order of the day in these permanently sunny climes.

in a hurry, you can find it. Also at the other extreme, lobster and all the trimmings can be indulged in surrounded by sumptuous decor.

Among the fine fish adorning the menu are snapper (similar to sea bream), John Dory, flounder, sole and whiting. News from the shellfish front is all good. Grilled or thermidored, lobster will make any occasion more festive. Or try delicious steamed mussels, fried prawns, Sydney rock oysters, or another local pride, Balmain bugs, relatives of the lobster family.

FOR CARNIVORES

High quality and hefty portions satisfy the most demanding meat-eaters. The choice, though, seems to boil down to steaks and chops, especially in the less elaborate restaurants, where meat pies might also be a good bet. If you're up to it, try carpetbag steak (stuffed with oysters). A warning to steak-lovers, however: no matter what kind of steak you order it will arrive well done unless you explain that you want it rare. If you feel strongly about this, emphasize that you want it 'blue' or it may well be incinerated.

In a country with ten times as many sheep as people, roast lamb and lamb chops are also in abundance. All sorts of meat are conducive to outdoor barbecueing, and as everybody knows, Australians just love their 'barbie'.

FRUIT AND VEGETABLES

Unusually, fresh Australian vegetables (often affectionately referred to as 'veggies') add flavour, wholesomeness and variety. Fruit is plentiful and delicious: the temperate zone provides apples, cherries, berries, and plums, while the tropics offer avocados, bananas, papayas (or pawpaws), passionfruit, pineapples and mangoes. Australia claims two great 'inventions' in the fruit department: the Granny Smith apple, originally cultivated by Maria Smith of Eastwood, NSW in the 1860s, and the William pear.

TO FOLLOW

A favourite Australian dessert is a light and fluffy meringue concoction traditionally topped with kiwi fruit, called a *pavlova*. It is named after Anna Pavlova, an immortal of the early 20th-century Russian ballet, who seems to have made a big impression when she visited Australia during a world tour. Another name-dropping dessert, *peach melba*, made with ice-cream and raspberry sauce, was dedicated to Melbourne's opera diva, Dame Nellie Melba. Calorific cakes and fruit pies come in many tempting flavours.

A wave of innovation has made Australian cheeses better than ever. Familiar cheddars are joined by ewe's-milk cheeses and others blended from cow's and goat's milk. From many parts of the country come pleasing imitations of Brie, Camembert, Gruyère, Gorgonzola and Gouda.

FOREIGN FOOD

Almost every small town in Australia has a foreign restaurant or two nowadays, feeding the ethnic population and of course the increasingly adventurous locals. Sydney carries this trend to its cosmopolitan

---

Bush Tucker

Natural food, Aboriginal style, includes a fabled delicacy, witchetty grubs, the larvae of beetles and moths found in trees and roots. In the bush they are eaten baked (at best), raw if necessary. Some brave visiting gourmets say witchetty grubs have a sweetish, nutty taste. Otherwise, the traditional staples include roast wallaby, snake or lizard, preferably with a garnish of various grasses, fruits, seeds and spices.

The sophistication of Sydney cuisine is a long way from the back of beyond, but you can try a taste of bush tucker at the Wattle Seed Deli, at Ultimo Road, Haymarket.

conclusion in a triumph of the Australian melting pot. You can choose from dozens of cultural cuisines, mostly from Europe and Asia. Chinese, Japanese, Thai, Korean and Indian styles of cooking are well represented, and you can never be sure what the next trend will be. The Vietnamese boat people of yesterday are now dishing up delicate, lettuce-wrapped spring rolls to an increasingly wider and appreciative audience.

Self-service establishments offer Chinese and Asian Smørgasbords, a reasonably priced way in which to discover *Shanghai sautéed prawns* and Thailand's *mee grob*; chopsticks are optional. At lunchtime, east and west meet in Chinese dim sum restaurants to sample their vast array of dumplings, buns and snacks.

Wine and Beer

They've been making wine in New South Wales since the dawn of civilization and it's getting better all the time.

One of the first projects ordered in 1788 by the founder of the New South Wales colony, Captain Phillip, was the planting of vines at Sydney Cove. Once Australians had developed a taste for home-grown wines, the demand became stronger throughout the country for fortified products like port and sherry.

Much later the people opened their hearts to the kind of still wines that complement a meal – a cool white, or a robust red. In recent years, experts have moved in to upgrade the more average wines by using the latest technology, propelling the best of the crop into the big leagues internationally.

Today, Australia is a world power in wine, with about 600 wineries supplying a nation that drinks twice as much wine per head as America or the United Kingdom. What's left over – something like 40 million litres – is exported to more than 80 countries, the most enthusiastic importing nations being Sweden, Britain and the United States.

HUNTER VALLEY

Only a day trip's distance from Sydney is an Australian wine region of now international renown, the Hunter Valley. Touring this equivalent of a châteaux is a rewarding experience, featuring tastings at the cellar door.

The Hunter Valley's reputation as a wine region is bigger than its output, which satisfies only a tiny percentage of the nation's needs. The district's most highly regarded wines are earthy reds from Shiraz grapes and dry Semillon whites. Other significant New South Wales wine dis-

Australian wines, long loved at home, have become increasingly accepted and respected in international circles.

tricts are Mudgee, Riverina and Upper Hunter.

Every state makes wine, even at the extremes in rainy Tasmania and the baking Northern Territory. The law of averages says you'll be offered wine from South Australia, which is the country's biggest producer (the Barossa Valley is its most famous district). Nationwide, white wine outsells red, with sweetish sparkling wines being particularly popular. Other options are rosé, sherry, port, vermouth, and some splendid Tokay and Muscat dessert wines.

THE 'AMBER NECTAR'

The first rule about Australian beer is that it must be chilled. In a drastic rejection of the old English tradition of tepid ales, the Australians like it cold enough to freeze the teeth and taste buds. Regardless of season, real beer fans use deep-frozen glasses, or enclose their cold 'tinnies' in insulated holders to defend them from the heat of the atmosphere.

Australian beer is widely exported. Foster's lager carries the flag to 80 thirsty countries. Other beers generate pronounced regional loyalties – for instance, Toohey's in New South Wales, Swan Lager in Western Australia and Castlemaine XXXX (called simply four-ex) in Queensland.

Australian beers, which are made in the pilsner or lager style, are stronger than their nearest equivalents from the USA or Britain, though some European brews contain even more alcohol.

Drinker's Glossary

bottle shop – liquor store or off-licence where bottles are sold to take away.

BYO – 'bring your own' bottle invitation from unlicensed restaurants.

cuppa – a cup of tea, if it should come to that.

esky – portable insulated cooler to carry beer, etc., to beach or barbecue.

tinnie – a tin (can) of beer.

BLUEPRINT
for a
Perfect Trip

An A-Z Summary of Practical Information

A

ACCOMMODATION (See also CAMPING, YOUTH HOSTELS)
Sydney welcomes travellers with every kind of accommodation from five-star palaces to austere economy-class rooms and backpackers' hostels. The luxury end of the spectrum is sumptuous in all respects and even in budget-priced hotel and motel rooms you can expect a private shower or bath, toilet, telephone, TV, refrigerator, and coffee- and tea-making equipment. Air conditioning (or at least a ceiling fan) is provided. You'll also come across plenty of bed and breakfast establishments.

A pleasant alternative is self-catering apartments with one, two or three bedrooms, maid service and fully-equipped kitchens, convenient for longer stays. (Many refuse one-night bookings, particularly at peak periods.)

Overseas offices of the Australian Tourist Commission have listings of hotels and motels. You can reserve accommodation through your travel agent or airline. Within Australia, book through the state tourist offices, domestic airlines and hotel chains. If you arrive out of the blue, the Travellers Information Service at the airport, or the New South Wales Travel Centre at 19 Castlereagh Street can help with last-minute reservations.

Accommodation may be hard to find when Australians themselves go travelling, by the million, during the school holidays. These are staggered state by state except for the year-end period when schools everywhere close. Offices of the Australian Tourist Commission have charts of the school holiday schedule more than a year in advance.

AIRPORTS

Sydney's Kingsford Smith Airport, 10 km (about 6 miles) from the city centre, is Australia's busiest international airport. Other principal gateways are Melbourne, Brisbane, Cairns, Darwin and Perth. Further international airports serve Adelaide, Hobart and Townsville. The domestic air network is highly developed, and even smallish towns usually have comfortable, efficient terminals.

Arriving passengers can travel from airport to town by taxi (10-20 minutes) or bus (20-30 minutes). The airport bus service goes to the door of major hotels. Note that the domestic and international terminals are a shuttle-bus ride apart.

BICYCLE HIRE

With clearly marked bicycle lanes, most Australian cities are attuned to cyclists. You can rent a bike in Sydney or the suburbs, or sign up for a tour including transport to and from a scenic area (bikes provided), food, accommodation, and the services of a guide.

CAMPING

Australians are avid campers, and you'll find campsites dotted all over. The sites tend to be packed during school holidays.

They have at least the basic amenities, and in some cases much more in the way of comfort. Aside from roomy tents with lights and floors, some installations have caravans (trailers) or cabins. Showers, toilets, laundry facilities and barbecue grills are commonly available. Sheets and blankets can often be hired. The national parks generally have well organized camping facilities. To camp beyond the designated zone you must ask the rangers for permission. There are coach tours for campers, or you can hire a campervan or motorhome by the day or week (see also CAR HIRE).

CAR HIRE

Having a car is really a burden in Sydney, with its traffic jams and parking problems. But there's no substitute for one when you want to see the Australian countryside at your own pace.

Brisk competition among the international and local car rental companies means you can often find economical rates or special deals, for instance unlimited mileage or weekend discounts. Rates will be considerably higher if you announce that you intend to drive in remote country areas. In general, it's worth shopping around. But be careful – some companies impose a metropolitan limit on vehicles. Check first, as your insurance won't be valid outside the designated area.

To rent a car you'll need a current Australian, overseas or International Driver's Licence. The minimum age is 21, or in some cases 25. Third-party insurance is automatically included; for an additional fee you can also sign up for collision damage and personal accident insurance.

You can pick up a car in one city and return it elsewhere. Interstate arrangements are commonly available from the big firms, which also have offices at airports. Campervans and caravans (trailers) are available, though most are reserved far in advance for school holiday periods.

If you're planning a long stay and a lot of travel, you could consider buying a car and selling it when you leave. It can, of course, be a complicated and risky business, even for an expert on used cars. However, a suburban Sydney firm, Mach 1 Autos (tel. 02/569 3374), has pioneered a seemingly fail-safe plan. It guarantees to buy back, at agreed prices, cars it has sold. If three or four people are travelling together, the scheme works out as a big saving.

CHILDREN'S AUSTRALIA

Between the beaches and the bush, the kangaroos and the koalas, Australia will keep children amused and amazed. In addition to the natural beauties and oddities, the man-made attractions rate highly: boat excursions, imaginative amusement parks and 'hands-on' interactive museums.

New latitudes bring new problems. Expert life-guards are present on all of Sydney's beaches, as are shark-protection devices and fully equipped first-aid stations, but elsewhere, in general, be sure to supervise children at the beaches at all times, as tides, sharks or poisonous jellyfish may be a menace. In the Outback, dangers can range from poisonous snakes and spiders to man-eating crocodiles. Seek local advice. On the 'plus' side, the standard of hygiene is high everywhere.

CLIMATE

The seasons, of course, are upside down from those in the Northern Hemisphere. Winter runs from June to August and the sun shines on Christmas Day. Sydney has a temperate climate with four seasons, all mild. In the New South Wales Outback, though, it's mostly very hot from December to February. From June to September you can expect the Snowy Mountains, in the south of the state, to live up to their name.

Statistics can lie or at least distort reality, but, for your general guidance, here are some average daily maximum and minimum Sydney temperatures, month by month:

	J	F	M	A	M	J	J	A	S	O	N	D
Max °C	26	26	25	22	19	17	16	18	20	22	24	25
Min °C	18	19	17	15	11	9	8	9	11	13	15	17
Max °F	79	79	77	72	66	63	61	64	68	72	75	77
Min °F	64	66	63	59	52	48	46	48	52	55	59	63
Sea temperature:												
°C	22	22	22	21	14	17	16	16	16	17	19	20
°F	72	72	72	70	58	63	61	61	61	63	66	68
Average number of days of traceable rainfall:												
	14	13	14	14	13	12	12	11	12	12	12	13

CLOTHING

Whatever your itinerary, whatever the season, forget an overcoat, although a sweater may come in handy, even in summer when, after a hot day in the sun, the evening breeze can seem downright chilly. A light raincoat will serve in almost any season. Anywhere you go you'll need comfortable walking shoes.

In Sydney, businessmen wear suits and ties except on hot summer days, when they put on short-sleeved shirts, walking shorts and long socks. They continue to put up with ties but abandon jackets. In less formal circumstances – sightseeing or shopping, for instance – both men and women wear shorts when it's warm. Some restaurants require jacket and tie, and even Outback restaurants and hotels may refuse clients with T-shirts, singlets and shorts or ripped jeans in the evening. Club regulations generally require a collared shirt and covered shoes – not runners or sandals.

COMPLAINTS

As Australia has no special agency to deal with complaints, your best bet is to work out any problems face to face with the shopkeeper, hotel manager or whoever is involved. If you think you've been overcharged or unfairly dealt with, the personal approach should be an effective remedy in plain-talking Australia. If not, try the Department of Consumer Affairs, 1 Oxford Street, Darlinghurst, tel. 02/286 0006.

CRIME

Although big crime remains a sensational rarity in Australia, and murders are few and far between, lesser crimes are steadily on the increase. As in most countries, it's wise to take precautions against burglary and petty theft. Have your valuables put into the hotel's safe deposit box. Lock your room and your car. Be on the alert for pickpockets on crowded buses and in markets.

Anti-drug laws vary greatly from state to state. Possession of cannabis or lesser drugs can mean up to two years in jail.

CUSTOMS, ENTRY AND EXIT FORMALITIES

All visitors, except New Zealanders, need valid passports and visas to enter Australia. Travel agencies and Australian consulates can provide visa application forms. The completed form, along with your passport and an identity photo, must be filed with the consulate. There is no charge for a visa. Only after a visa has been issued should you buy your air ticket.

Travellers issued with the normal short-term visitor visa are formally warned that it precludes their getting a job or undertaking a course of studies while in Australia, much less becoming a permanent resident. However, 18-to-25-year-olds can apply for a working holiday visa, normally valid for six months, permitting casual employment. Unaccompanied children under 18 must have the written consent of a parent or guardian.

Entry formalities. On the last leg of your flight to Australia you'll be asked to complete a voluminous customs form, swearing that you are not trying to import foreign foodstuffs, weapons, drugs or other forbidden articles. The checklist runs to 15 categories of prohibited items. There is also an Immigration form. If you're arriving in Australia after a stop in an area where yellow fever is endemic, you must show a valid vaccination certificate. You'll also have to show your return or onward ticket, and you may need to prove that your funds are sufficient to last out your planned stay.

Exit formalities. Leaving Australia, each passenger aged 12 or over must pay a $20 departure tax. (If you've run out of cash by then, major credit cards are accepted.) Alternatively you can buy a departure tax stamp from most post offices to avoid queues at the airport. Children under 12 must obtain an exemption sticker from the Departure Tax counter at the airport, for which proof of age is required. One final bit of business to keep the bureaucratic wheels turning: a departure form to fill in for the Immigration authorities.

Duty-free. The chart on the following page shows the main duty-free items you may take into Australia and, when returning home, into your own country.

Into:	Cigarettes		Cigars		Tobacco	Spirits		Wine
Australia	200	or	250 g	or	250 g	1 L	and	1 L
Canada	200	and	50	and	900 g	1.1 L	or	1.1 L
Eire	200	and	50	or	250 g	1 L	and	2 L
New Zealand	200	or	50	or	250 g	1.1 L	and	4.5 L
South Africa	400	and	50	and	250 g	1 L	and	2 L
UK	200	or	50	or	250 g	1 L	and	2 L
USA	200	and	100	and	*	1 L	or	1 L

* a reasonable quantity

D

DISABLED TRAVELLERS

People with special needs get sympathetic treatment in all areas of Australian life but only the newer buildings are equipped with wheelchair ramps and other facilities. It's always best to give advance notice of your requirements to hotels, airlines, etc. For information about the places geared to people with special needs, write to the Australia Council for Rehabilitation for the Disabled (ACROD), PO Box 60, Curtin, ACT 2605; tel. 062/82 4333. The Sydney City Council (tel. 02/267 1437) issues a map highlighting accessible places.

DRIVING IN AUSTRALIA

Like Britain and many Asian countries, Australia upholds tradition by driving on the left. Australian roads are good, considering the size of the country and the problems of distance, terrain and climate. Although the most populous regions have ever more freeways (expressways or motorways – some of them beautifully landscaped), most country roads are two-lane highways which are often over-crowded at busy times.

Regulations. Drive on the left and pass on the right. Drivers and passengers must wear seat belts. The speed limit in cities and towns is 60 kmph (about 35 mph). In the N.S.W. countryside, the limit is 100 kmph (about 60 mph). Driving under the influence of alcohol or drugs is a serious offence. Spot checks are made, with breath tests. The limit on alcohol in the blood is .05%, meaning in practice that three drinks will take you over the top.

City driving. Heavy traffic and parking problems afflict the downtown area, which may help to explain why Sydney drivers are so impatient. Parking meters and 'no standing' zones proliferate. For longer stays parking garages are the answer, but these, too, fill up.

Outback driving. Check thoroughly the condition of your car and be sure you have a spare wheel. Find out about the fuel situation in advance and leave word as to your destination and anticipated arrival time. Always have plenty of drinking water in the car. Fill up the fuel tank at every opportunity, for the next station may be a few hundred kilometres away. Some dirt roads are so smooth you may be tempted to speed, but conditions can change abruptly; also, soft shoulders and clouds of dust are problems when other vehicles pass. Be particularly cautious with road trains, consisting of three or four huge trailers barrelling down the highway towed by a high-powered truck. Pass one, if you dare, with the greatest of care.

Fuel. Many filling stations are open only during normal shopping hours, so you may have to ask where out-of-hours service is available. Petrol in most garages comes in super, unleaded-regular and unleaded-super grades and is dispensed by the litre. Most stations are self-service.

Road signs. Signposting is generally good, especially along heavily used roads. All distances are measured in kilometres. Tourist attractions and natural wonders are signalled by white-on-brown direction signs. To drive into the centre of any city, simply follow the signs marked 'City'. But leaving a city is less straightforward: exit routes are often signposted with the assumption that every driver has local experience, so you may require a good map and some advance planning. Although most road signs are the standard international **117**

pictographs, many use words. Some of these may confuse even English-speakers:

crest	steep hilltop limiting visibility
cyclist hazard	dangerous for cyclists
dip	severe depression in road surface
hump	bump or speed obstacle
safety ramp	uphill escape lane from steep downhill road
soft edges	soft shoulders

E

ELECTRIC CURRENT
The standard throughout Australia is 240-250 volt, 50 cycle AC. Three-pronged plugs, in the shape of a bird's footprint, are universal, so you should take an adaptor. Most hotel rooms also have 110-volt outlets for razors and small appliances.

EMBASSIES AND CONSULATES
The embassies or high commissions of about 70 countries are established in Canberra, the national capital. They have consular sections dealing with passport renewal, visas and other formalities. More than 40 countries also maintain diplomatic outposts in Sydney, which can be useful for citizens in difficulty. To find the address of your consulate, look in the white pages of the telephone directory under 'Consuls' or in the *Yellow Pages* under 'Consulates and Legations'.

EMERGENCIES
Ambulance – Fire – Police: Dial 000.
The 000 number – no coin required from public telephones – is in service in all cities and most towns. If you're in a remote area, however, look for the emergency numbers inside the front cover of the local telephone directory.

ETIQUETTE

In Australia's informal, egalitarian atmosphere, people usually introduce themselves by their first name, even in business relationships. (Don't be shocked if the motel receptionist calls you by your first name, either.) In spite of the relaxed atmosphere, punctuality is the order of the day, and visitors are expected to follow the rules.

Australians are eminently approachable and convivial people, so you can strike up a conversation almost anywhere – at a bus stop, at the beach or in a pub. One way to get close to the people is to stay in bed and breakfast accommodation in family homes.

Many areas of the country – and not only in the Outback – contain places or things that have special meaning to the Aborigines. These 'sacred sites' are protected by law. Visitors should show sensitivity and consideration for their historical significance.

GETTING TO SYDNEY

BY AIR

Flights from Asia, North America and Europe serve nine international airports around Australia, of which Sydney's is the busiest. APEX and other special fares reduce the expense of travelling such great distances. Look into round-the-world fares as well. Travel agents have information on a big range of package tours available – fly-drive arrangements, rail or bus tours, camping holidays and safaris.

Getting to Australia by any route is a long haul. Fastest journey times are New York-Sydney 22 hours, Los Angeles-Sydney 15 hours, London-Sydney 21 hours. If jet-lag is a factor, consider breaking the flight for a day or two at one of the stops along the way; in most cases this doesn't affect the price of the air ticket.

BY SEA

A number of Australian ports feature in the itineraries of cruise ships. You can fly to, say, Bali or Fiji and embark on the liner there, sail to Australia, then fly home from any Australian city, or resume the cruise at another port.

GUIDES AND TOURS

Several tour companies offer a broad choice of excursions, from half a day in Sydney to long-haul journeys into the Outback. Harbour cruises range from the general sightseeing tour to specialized visits to historic Fort Denison. There are also local walking tours, for instance around The Rocks, and tours for cyclists, wildlife-lovers and others catering to special interests. Brochures are available at your hotel or the tourist office. Long-distance coach tours are very popular among Australians as well as foreign visitors. The coach drivers generally contribute a running commentary rich in facts and folksy humour. On tours of two or more days, the main meals are included in the price, along with accommodation in hotels or motels along the way. Round-Australia coach tours, which touch every mainland state, can go on for nearly two months.

H

HITCH HIKING

Although discouraged by the authorities (and banned on freeways and everywhere in Queensland), hitch-hiking is fairly commonplace in Australia, even in isolated spots where prospects are few. Successful practitioners recommend you display a sign with your destination clearly marked. It helps to choose an effective location, usually on the outskirts of a town, where cars and trucks go slowly and can pull over easily and safely.

L

LANGUAGE

Australian is spoken everywhere in the nation. The vernacular is called *Strine*, which is the way the word 'Australian' sounds in an extreme Australian pronunciation. It is spoken in what the uninitiated may take for a profound Cockney accent piped through the nose. Foreigners who listen carefully usually understand what's said, at least when it's repeated (see cover flap for a few examples).

In addition to English, a host of foreign languages serve the immigrant communities. Special multicultural radio stations broadcast in more than 50 languages. Non-English speakers with problems can get help from the Telephone Interpreter System (TIS), which is able to translate on telephone calls to doctors or emergency services. Interpreters on call can handle many languages including French, German, Greek, Italian and Spanish. They operate round the clock in the bigger cities, for the price of a local phone call. The TIS number for Sydney is 02/221 1111. For Canberra and outside major cities telephone 008 11 2477 or 008 33 3330.

LAUNDRY AND DRY CLEANING

Hotels and motels usually offer same-day laundry and dry-cleaning service for guests, though it tends to be quite expensive. Ask the receptionist, porter or maid. Many hotels and motels also have do-it-yourself washers and dryers on the premises.

LOST PROPERTY

If you've lost something, your hotel receptionist can probably tell you where to find the relevant Lost and Found department. In Sydney there is one Lost Property Office for things lost in taxis, and another for property left behind in buses, trains and ferries. Otherwise, try the police.

MAPS

State and local tourist offices give away useful maps of their areas, and there are free specialized maps – of Darling Harbour, for instance, or the Sydney ferry network. For more detailed maps, check at news-stands and bookstores. Car hire companies often supply free city directories showing each street and place of interest.

MEDICAL CARE

Standards of hygiene are high throughout Australia and, in fact, you can drink the tap water anywhere – unless a notice specifically warns otherwise. However, there are hazards at the seaside and in the countryside, starting with the threat of too much sun. Skin cancer has become a serious concern in sun-worshipping Australia; protective cream is essential, even on cloudy days.

Further afield, poisonous snakes and spiders lurk in many places, and bathers must beware of sharks and, in certain seasons and areas, dangerous jellyfish. In the north, crocodiles are a genuine menace. Also, at the beach, watch where you walk – and swim. Some of Sydney's beaches have suffered pollution problems, but since the recent ocean cleanup programmes, there has been a great improvement. The state of the waters is announced daily in the newspapers and on the radio.

Australia has excellent medical services, with highly trained doctors and fully equipped modern hospitals, but the fees are high. Visitors are well advised to arrange in advance for insurance to cover any medical or hospital costs on the trip. Your hotel can call a doctor if you fall ill, or you can get a list of approved doctors from your embassy, high commission or consulate.

If you have a doctor's prescription from your own doctor or physician overseas it cannot be taken care of by an Australian pharmacy unless you have it endorsed by a local doctor. There are late-night chemists in various districts of Sydney, especially in the King's Cross district. For the address of an all-night pharmacy, telephone 02/438 3333.

MONEY MATTERS

Currency: Since 1966, when pounds, shillings and pence were abandoned, the monetary unit has been the Australian dollar (abbreviated $ or $A), divided into 100 cents. There are coins of 5, 10, 20 and 50 cents, $1 and $2. Banknotes come in denominations of $5, $10, $20, $50 and $100. You can bring with you as much Australian or foreign currency as you wish, and on departure you can take away $5,000 in local currency.

Changing money: Exchange rates fluctuate daily. Traveller's cheques and foreign currency may be changed at most banks in Australia with a minimum of fuss. Some states charge a small tax for each transaction. Many hotels will change money at all hours, but the rate tends to be unfavourable.

Credit cards: The well-known international credit cards are recognized by car rental companies, airlines, hotels, in most restaurants and stores, and in most tourist spots.

N

NEWSPAPERS AND MAGAZINES

More than 500 newspapers are published in Australia, from internationally esteemed big-city dailies like the *Sydney Morning Herald* (the oldest newspaper in the southern hemisphere) to backwoods weeklies. As in the United States, papers have traditionally served local communities or states rather than a nationwide readership. The first national newspaper, Rupert Murdoch's *The Australian*, was founded in 1964. Dozens of periodicals aimed at the immigrant communities are published in Dutch, French, German, Greek, Italian and other languages. In Sydney specialist news-stands sell newspapers airlifted from London, Rome, Paris, Hong Kong and Singapore as well as weekly and monthly American and European magazines.

O

OPENING HOURS

Banks are open from 9.30am to 4pm Monday to Thursday, and until 5pm Friday. Certain key ones are also open on Saturdays now. Some big banks open at 8.15am and close at 5pm for foreign currency exchange. The bank at Sydney Airport is open until 11pm seven days a week.

Post offices: Most are open 9am to 5pm. Monday to Friday, but the Sydney GPO operates 8.15am to 5.30pm Monday to Friday, and 8.30am to 12 noon Saturday.

Shopping: The big department stores are open from 9am to 5.30pm Monday to Friday and from 9am to 4pm on Saturday. Thursday is late shopping night when stores stay open until 8 or 9pm. Shopping centres like the Queen Victoria Building and Harbourside are open seven days a week.

Offices: 9am to 5pm Monday to Friday.

Bars/pubs/hotels: Licensing hours vary, but a typical schedule would be 10am to 10pm Monday to Saturday, with some places open after noon on Sundays. Nightclubs carry on until 3am, some functioning 24 hours a day in King's Cross.

Museums: 10am to 5pm Monday to Saturday, noon to 5pm Sunday.

P

PHOTOGRAPHY

There's so much to focus on that you'll probably run out of film. No problem, though: internationally known brands are sold everywhere in Australia. Quick-processing establishments can be found in all the cities.

In the desert and the tropics, make sure you keep your camera and film well out of the hot sun, and beware of the ever-invading sand, dust and moisture.

Many Aborigines resent having their photos taken – the advice is to ask before you aim. Some Aboriginal sites, even well-known landmarks, are sensitive subjects for filming, so don't make a scene if you're waved away.

Wildlife is a fascinating subject, but it's only prudent to keep your distance when, for example, crocodiles or wild boar appear in the viewfinder. And it's worth remembering that buffalo can be far more dangerous than they appear.

PLANNING YOUR BUDGET

To give you an idea of what to expect, here are some average prices in Australian dollars. However, these can only be approximate in view of the problem of inflation.

Air fares: Sydney-Adelaide-Sydney economy $498, 'See Australia' fare $374; Sydney-Melbourne economy $136.

Airport transfer: Sydney Airport to city – coach: $4, taxi: $10-12.

Car hire: Economy (unlimited kilometres): $59 per day plus $12 insurance, $357 per week plus $70 insurance. Business class: $89 per day, $532 per week (insurance included). Luxury class: $200-250 per day, $1,000-1,500 per week. Monthly rates also available.

Cigarettes: $2.50 for 20, $2.80-3.00 for 30.

Coach tour: Half day $20-35, full day $50-70.

Hairdressers:. Ladies' haircut $25-30, shampoo and set $15-20. Men's cut $15-20.

Hotels: Double room: luxury $250-$550 per night; premium $120-$300; moderate $70-$120; budget $30-$65.

Meals and drinks: In a moderate restaurant, lunch $25, dinner $35. Bottle of wine (from bottle shop) $7-20, beer $2, soft drink 80c-$1.20.

Nightlife: Nightclub, cover charge or minimum $5-15; concert $35 and up; theatre $25 and up; cinema $12.

Sydney Explorer Bus: Adults $15, children $10, family $30.

Taxis: Circular Quay to King's Cross $10.

Trains: Sydney-Brisbane first-class $130; berth $151, economy $79; 14-day economy Austrail pass $415 (budget), $690 first class.

POLICE

Each state (and the Northern Territory) operates its own police force, covering both urban and rural areas. The Australian Federal Police, based in Canberra, has jurisdiction over government property, including airports, and deals with interstate problems like drugs and organized crime.

POST OFFICES

Australia's 4,500 post offices are signposted 'Australia Post'. Most adhere to a 9am to 5pm schedule Monday to Friday, though Sydney's historic General Post Office (GPO) opens from 8.15am to 5.30pm and also Saturday morning until 12 noon. Letterboxes throughout Australia are red with a horizontal white stripe.

If you don't know exactly where you'll be staying, you can have letters addressed to you c/o Poste Restante or to the Post Office Delivery Desk at the General Post Office. You'll have to show identification when you pick up your mail. At Sydney's GPO the Poste Restante bureau is computerized: type in your name (there are instructions in six languages), and if mail awaits you the machine prints out a ticket; take it to the window, where a human will hand over your letter.

Telegrams and cablegrams can be sent from any post office or dictated over the phone from your hotel or motel room. Most post offices have telex and fax facilities, as do hotels.

PUBLIC HOLIDAYS

January 1	New Year's Day
April 25	Anzac Day
December 25	Christmas Day
December 26	Boxing Day
Moveable dates:	Australia Day (Monday closest to Jan 26)
	Good Friday
	Easter Saturday
	Easter Monday
	Queen's Birthday

Certain other public holidays are celebrated only in certain states or a single region, while still other holidays are observed at different times in different states: Labour Day comes any time between March and October, according to where you are, but in Sydney it's the first

Monday in October. School holidays come four times a year, the longest one being in the summer, tending to swamp hotels and tourist attractions.

PUBLIC TRANSPORT
LOCAL:

Buses are more practical (if more crowded) during business hours (frequencies taper off after dark). There are two main starting points for buses: the Wynard Park terminus in York Street for northern suburbs, and the Circular Quay area for buses heading elsewhere. The fare depends on the distance travelled; tickets may be purchased from the driver or from bus company operatives at the main stops. A free city bus, route 777, follows a circular route around the central district. Another free bus, 666, links the Wynyard station and the Art Gallery.

Passes. There are special tickets valid for unlimited public transport travel for two hours or a whole day. State Transit offers a 3-day SydneyPass which includes all normal bus and ferry services, Sydney Explorer, Airport Express Bus, Rocks/Darling Harbour shuttle bus and all three Sydney Ferries cruises, for $39.

Sydney's **underground railway** system (subway), operating from 4.30am to midnight, serves as the central portion of a railway network stretching out to the suburbs. Follow the colour-coded route system, checking the departure signs in the stations and on platforms.

Sydney's **monorail**, more a prototype of a futuristic transport system than a serious means of getting around, scenically links the central city and Darling Harbour. It shuts down at 9 p.m.

Ferries, which sail between 6am and 11pm daily, are a vital part of life in Sydney, with so many commuters crossing the harbour. The ferries, concentrated at Circular Quay, also provide cheap outings for sightseers to Kirribilli or Neutral Bay, or, more touristically, to Taronga Zoo. Ferries or fast JetCats shuttle between Circular Quay and Manly. And the slow but scenic way from Circular Quay to Darling Harbour is by ferry.

Water taxis let you set your own itinerary. Phone 02/922 4252.

INTERCITY:

Domestic flights. Air traffic is exceptionally well developed, with more than 14 million passengers a year flying the domestic airlines across Australia's vastness. It's wise to make advance reservations, particularly during the busy school holiday periods. Tourists from overseas are entitled to discounts on air tickets, but the packages may involve rigid itineraries. Well-informed travel agents can supply details of the latest deals.

Trains. Intercity train travel in Australia can be a great adventure. The legendary journeys are between Adelaide and Alice Springs (22 hours on the *Ghan*) and between Sydney and Perth (65 hours aboard the *Indian-Pacific*). Modern air-conditioned trains with sleeping compartments, showers, dining cars and club cars cover these gruelling routes in comfort. Advance reservations – up to 12 months in advance – are especially recommended for the *Indian-Pacific*. On a more prosaic level, trains cover shorter-range interstate and commuter runs. Ask a travel agent about money-saving rail passes, in first or economy class, for foreign tourists.

Intercity buses. Luxurious air-conditioned express coaches, often equipped with everything from toilets to television, link all the main cities. For unhurried travellers who want to see Australia close up, at a reasonable price, the main coach companies offer special bargain deals, for instance two weeks or a month of unlimited mileage at fixed rates. Some of the packages must be purchased before you arrive in Australia. To give you an idea of what you're in for, Sydney to Adelaide is a 24-hour trip.

R

RADIO AND TV

Government-funded stations of the Australian Broadcasting Commission (ABC) and the Special Broadcasting Service (SBS) compete with a range of commercially run stations. Sydney has five television channels operating from 6am to midnight or later. The

SBS stations are devoted to 'multicultural' programmes, primarily in foreign languages with English subtitles. Sydney has a profusion of AM and FM radio stations for all tastes. The output of ABC-FM is almost entirely composed of classical music. Short-wave listeners can pick up Radio Australia (the overseas service of the ABC) and other long-range broadcasters such as the Voice of America, BBC World Service and Asian stations.

RELIGION

The majority religion in Australia is Christianity. The biggest denominations are Anglican (Church of England) and Roman Catholic, followed by Uniting Church, Presbyterian and Orthodox. Of the non-Christian faiths, Muslims are the largest group, followed by Jews and Buddhists. To find the church of your choice, check at your hotel desk or look in the *Yellow Pages* of the telephone directory under 'Churches and Synagogues'.

RESTAURANTS

See EATING OUT and HOTELS AND RESTAURANTS sections.

SMOKING

On public transport – including all domestic flights – in theatres and lifts or elevators, as well as in government offices, smoking is strictly prohibited. Some hotels and restaurants have established smoke-free zones.

Smokers can find a big selection of Australian and imported cigarettes on sale everywhere. They come in packs of 20, 25 or 30. Specialist shops also stock a plethora of imported cigars and pipe tobacco. Prices vary from state to state.

TAXIS

You can hail a taxi on the street if the bright orange light on top is lit. Otherwise go to one of the cab stands, usually found at shopping centres, transport terminals and big hotels, and take the first taxi in the rank. Or alternatively phone for a taxi on, for instance, 332 8888 or 897 4000. Meters indicate the fare plus any extras, such as waiting time. A courtesy note: Australians usually sit next to the taxi driver, but if you prefer the back seat, no offence is generally taken.

TELEPHONES

The Telecom Australia network is highly sophisticated; from almost any phone, even in the Outback, you can dial anywhere in the country, and the signal is loud and clear. Many hotel rooms have phones from which you can dial cross-country (STD) or internationally (IDD). Some hotels add a surcharge to your telephone bill.

There are four kinds of coin-operated telephones. Green, gold and blue phones accept 10c, 20c, 50c and $1 coins and may be used for IDD or STD calls as well as local numbers. Red phones are for local calls only; put 30c in the slot. Some public telephones accept credit cards. There is a payphone centre at 100 King Street, Sydney, open 24 hours a day.

Telephone directories give full instructions on dialling and details on emergency and other services. To reach an overseas number, dial 0011, then the country code of the destination, the area code and the local number. (Dialling *to* Australia from overseas, the country code is 61.)

TIME DIFFERENCES

Australia is so big it needs three time zones: Eastern, Central and Western. Awkwardly, Central time is only half an hour earlier than Eastern, and daylight saving time occurs (but not in all states) during the northern hemisphere's winter. Here is the outlook for the period **130** from March to October when Australia is on standard time:

Los Angeles	New York	London	Perth	Adelaide	Sydney
4am	7am	noon	7pm	8.30pm	9pm

TIPPING

For most foreigners, the Australian view of tipping takes some getting used to. Virtually no one in the service sector of the economy expects to be tipped. Nobody's livelihood depends on tips. A gratuity is optional, a reward for good service but not a requirement.

In hotels frequented by foreigners, however, porters are accustomed to receiving tips. In good restaurants a tip of 5-10% is a just reward for efficient, courteous service. Taxi drivers accept but don't expect tips. But it certainly won't hurt any feelings if you *do* give a tip in appreciation.

TOILETS

Australians manage without euphemisms for 'toilet', though in a country so rich in slang you won't be surprised to come across some wry synonyms. When you find them, the facilities are often distinguished by the letters 'M' and 'F' for Male and Female. Public conveniences usually adhere to a high standard of cleanliness and comfort, even in the Outback.

TOURIST INFORMATION OFFICES

Some overseas offices of the Australian Tourist Commission (ATC):
USA: 31st Floor, 489 Fifth Ave, New York, NY 10017; tel. (212) 687-6300. Suite 2130, 150 N. Michigan Ave, Chicago, IL 60601; tel. (312) 781-5150. Suite 1200, 2121 Avenue of the Stars, Los Angeles, CA 90067; tel. (213) 552-1988.
Canada: Suite 1730, 2 Bloor Street West, Toronto, Ontario M4W 3E2; tel. (416) 925-9597.
UK: Gemini House, 8-10 Putney Hill, Putney, London SW15; tel. (081) 780 1424.
New Zealand: 15th Floor, Quay Towers, 29 Customs Street West, Auckland 1; tel. (09) 79 9594.

Singapore: 17th Floor, United Square, 101 Thompson Road, Singapore 1103; tel. (65) 255-4555.

Hong Kong: Sun Plaza Suite 604-605, Canton Road, Tsimshatsui, Kowloon, Hong Kong; tel. 311 1555.

Japan: Sankaido Building, 8th Floor, 9-13 Akasaka 1-chome, Minato-ku, Tokyo 107; tel. (03) 582 2191.

In Sydney, the NSW Travel Centre is at 19 Castlereagh Street, tel. 02/231 4444. The office is full of booklets, maps and information, and can help you with arrangements for travel and accommodation. At Sydney International Airport, the Travellers' Information Service operates seven days a week from 5am to 11pm, tel. 02/669 5111.

VACCINATIONS

Unless you are stopping in an infected area on your way, no vaccinations are required for entering Australia from the US, Canada or Europe.

WATER

Yes, you can drink the water from the tap in any Australian town, unless it's specifically marked otherwise. In the Outback, warnings might read 'Bore water' or 'Not for drinking'.

WEIGHTS AND MEASURES

Since the 1960s, Australia has adhered to the metric system's kilometres and kilogrammes, litres and metres, and the Celsius temperature system has taken over from Fahrenheit. Old-timers may still reckon distances in miles, but except for proverbs and poetry, the abandonment of British Imperial measures is total.

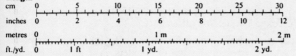

Temperature

| °C | 30 | 25 | 20 | 15 | 10 | 5 | 0 | 5 | 10 | 15 | 20 | 25 | 30 | 35 | 40 | 45 |
| °F | −20 | −10 | 0 | 10 | 20 | 30 | 40 | 50 | 60 | 70 | 80 | 90 | 100 | 110 |

Length

| cm | 0 | | 5 | | 10 | | 15 | | 20 | | 25 | | 30 |
| inches | 0 | | 2 | | 4 | | 6 | | 8 | | 10 | | 12 |

| metres | 0 | 1 m | 2 m |
| ft./yd. | 0 | 1 ft | 1 yd. | 2 yd. |

Weight

| grams | 0 | 100 | 200 | 300 | 400 | 500 | 600 | 700 | 800 | 900 | 1 kg |
| ounces | 0 | 4 | 8 | 12 | 1 lb. | 20 | 24 | 28 | 2 lb. |

Fluid measures

| imp.gals. | 0 | 5 | 10 |

| litres | 0 | 5 | 10 | 20 | 30 | 40 | 50 |

| U.S.gals. | 0 | 5 | 10 |

Kilometres to miles

| km | 0 | 1 | 2 | 3 | 4 | 5 | 6 | 8 | 10 | 12 | 14 | 16 |
| miles | 0 | ½ | 1 | 1½ | 2 | 3 | 4 | 5 | 6 | 7 | 8 | 9 | 10 |

Y

YOUTH HOSTELS

Young backpackers should have a membership card from the Youth Hostel Association in their home country. Information may be obtained from the Australian Youth Hostel Association, 60 Mary Street, Surry Hills, NSW 2010; tel. 02/212 1266.

For alternative accommodation at extremely economical rates, there are several chains of backpacker hostels unaffiliated with the YHA. Standards and facilities vary greatly. Detailed directories are available.

Index

Where there is more than one page reference, the one in bold refers to the main entry, those in italic refer to photographs.